International Trade and FDI

International Trade and FDI

An Advanced Introduction to Regulation and Facilitation

Warnock Davies and Clive G. Chen

BEP

BUSINESS EXPERT PRESS

Leader in applied, concise business books

International Trade and FDI: An Advanced Introduction to Regulation and Facilitation

First published in 2023 by
Business Expert Press, LLC
222 East 46th Street, New York, NY 10017
www.businessexpertpress.com

ISBN-13: 978-1-63742-504-6 (paperback)
ISBN-13: 978-1-63742-505-3 (e-book)

Business Expert Press International Business Collection

First edition: 2023

10 9 8 7 6 5 4 3 2 1

Description

This book is for use in IMBA, MIB, LLM, and other graduate programs; in university-based executive development programs; and in in-company seminars—and for use as a handbook and reference book by managers, executives, board members, consultants, and legal counsel who are engaged in the practice of international trade and/or foreign direct investment (FDI).

The book provides an advanced introduction to the governmental, intergovernmental, and non-governmental factors that regulate and facilitate the conduct of international trade and FDI. These factors include:

- Tariff barriers, non-tariff barriers, and other barriers to trade;
- Entry and post-entry barriers to FDI;
- Provisions contained in the GATT and other international trade instruments;
- The functionalities of the WTO, other global mechanisms, and regional trade blocks; and
- International standards, the harmonization of laws, and the settlement of disputes.

The material in the book is drawn from multiple disciplines, which include international relations, international trade, international law, and economic and diplomatic history; relies primarily on original source materials; makes extensive use of examples; and is formatted to facilitate its use as a textbook, handbook, and reference book.

Keywords

international trade; foreign direct investment; international business; international law; international management; international commerce; World Trade Organization; preferential trade agreement; free trade area; customs union; trade barriers; graduate programs; executive development

Contents

Preface

This book provides an advanced introduction to the governmental, inter-governmental, and non-governmental factors that regulate and facilitate the conduct of international trade and foreign direct investment (FDI). These factors include: tariff barriers, non-tariff barriers, and other barriers to trade; entry barriers and post-entry barriers to FDI; provisions contained in the General Agreement on Tariffs and Trade (GATT), in other global instruments, and in regional and bilateral preferential trade agreements; the functionalities of the World Trade Organization (WTO), other global mechanisms, and regional trade blocks—which include free trade areas and customs unions; and international standards, the harmonization of laws, and the settlement of disputes.

Design, Uses, Terms, and Format

The book was designed and written for use in IMBA, MIB, LLM, and other graduate programs; in university-based executive development programs; and in in-company seminars—and for use as a handbook and reference book by managers, executives, board members, consultants, and legal counsel who are engaged in the practice of international trade and/or FDI.

The material covered in the book is drawn from multiple fields, which include international relations, international commerce, international law, and economic and diplomatic history. The book relies primarily on original source materials, which are cited and listed in the bibliography, and makes extensive use of examples.

The terms used in the book are those used in the GATT, other WTO instruments, and non-WTO global instruments; terms used by the WTO and other global mechanisms; and terms that are in general usage in the field of international commerce. Where there is an inconsistency in the use of terms from these sources (such as the WTO and general usage of the initialism PTA), or where there is a difference between a term used by these sources and the term used by the US government (such as *most-favored-nation* or *normal value*), the inconsistency or difference is noted in the text.

To facilitate the book's use in graduate and executive programs and seminars—and as a handbook and reference book by managers, executives, board members, consultants, and legal counsel—the format uses four levels of headings and subheadings, short paragraphs, and vertical lists; the examples are separated from the body of the text; and the bibliography listings include URLs. Also, headings and subheadings have been numbered to facilitate cross-referencing, and footnotes are used to cross-reference key terms, concepts, principles, sources, and subject areas.

The US Edition

The concepts and principles discussed in the book are universal, but the examples are edition specific. More than half of the examples in this United States (US) edition refer to international trade occurring between the US and other countries or customs territories; to FDI by a US commercial entity, or to FDI in the US; to global, regional, or bilateral instruments or mechanisms that include US participation; or to other situations (such as international standards or commercial disputes) that involve the US government, a US state or municipal government, or a US non-governmental or commercial entity.

Warnock Davies and Clive G. Chen

PART I

Introduction

CHAPTER 1

The Fundamental Divisions

Contents

1.1   International Trade and FDI

All commercial activities can be classified as either domestic or international. All international commercial activities can be classified as either *international trade* or *foreign direct investment* (FDI).

International trade and FDI are discrete elements, but more than one-third of world trade occurs between commercial entities and their FDI subsidiaries, or between an entity's FDI subsidiaries; and 80 percent of world trade is by entities that are engaged in FDI.

1.1.1   External Trade and International Trade

The term *trade* refers to the sale and delivery, or purchase and delivery, of products or services. "The General Agreement on Tariffs and Trade" (GATT)[1] refers to trade activity that crosses the border of a nation-state[2]

---

[1] All references to the GATT that do not specify a year are to GATT 1994 (which includes GATT 1947). This is discussed in Chapter 8, Section 8.4.3.2.

[2] The term *nation-state* is discussed in Chapter 7, Section 7.1.1. In the field of international commerce, references to nations, states, nation-states, and countries include separate customs territories. Separate customs territories are discussed in Chapter 7, Section 7.1.3.

as *importation* and *exportation*, and as *imports* and *exports*,[3] and refers to these collectively as *external trade*.

Trade activity that occurs between nation-states is referred to as *international trade*. The distinction between *external trade* and *international trade* is that: (1) the term *external trade* is used when referring to imports into a nation-state and/or exports from a nation-state; (2) the term *international trade* is used when referring to trade between nation-states.

1.1.2   Foreign Direct Investment

There is no generally accepted definition of the term *foreign direct investment*—because the criteria that define FDI are set by the government of each host country.[4] There is, however, general agreement that foreign direct investment refers to an investment that is made in a nation-state by an individual or entity that is a national of another nation-state.[5]

Definitions of FDI can also include specific qualitative and quantitative criteria. For example, the Organization of Economic Cooperation and Development (OECD) benchmark defines FDI as "a category of cross-border investment" that is made for the purpose of "establishing a lasting interest in an enterprise," where "the direct investor owns at least 10 percent of the voting power of the direct investment enterprise," and where the level of equity ownership provides the foreign investor with "significant influence or control" of the enterprise.[6] Some definitions of FDI also include investment by an individual or entity that is a national of the nation-state that is the location of the investment, but is a resident of another nation-state or separate customs territory. The term *foreign direct investment* is discussed further in Chapter 5, Section 5.2.

---

[3] GATT, Article I, Paragraph 1.
[4] The term *host country* is discussed in Chapter 7, Section 7.1.2.1.
[5] Individual and corporate nationality is discussed in Chapter 7, Section 7.1.4.
[6] The OECD Benchmark Definition of FDI is discussed in Chapter 5, Section 5.2.1.

1.1.3 Foreign Portfolio Investment

The term *foreign portfolio investment* (FPI)[7] refers to the ownership of equity in an enterprise, where: (1) the nationality of the investor who owns the equity interest is different from the nationality of the enterprise, and (2) the level of equity ownership does not provide the foreign investor with "significant influence or control"[8] of the enterprise. Because of the absence of significant influence or control, FPI is generally not considered to be an international commercial activity. For these reasons, and the reasons covered in Chapter 5, Sections 5.2 through 5.2.1.2, the discussion of foreign investment in this book is focused solely on FDI.

1.2   The Factor Categories

The conduct of international trade and FDI is affected by market and nonmarket forces. The nonmarket forces include governmental, intergovernmental, and non-governmental factors—which can be grouped into two primary categories: (1) regulating factors and (2) facilitating factors.

1.2.1   Regulating Factors

The factors that regulate the conduct of international trade and FDI include the policies, laws, regulations, requirements, decisions, and actions by the governments of single nation-states. Factors that restrict or regulate the conduct of international commerce are referred to as *barriers*—which can be classified as either *trade barriers* or *investment barriers*.

Trade barriers are also called *barriers to trade*. A trade barrier is any factor that restricts or regulates external trade to or from a nation-state, separate customs territory, free trade area, or customs union. Most trade barriers are governmental, but some non-governmental factors act as barriers to trade. Trade barriers include three subcategories: (1) tariff barriers, (2) non-tariff barriers, and (3) other barriers to trade.

---

[7] In some countries, FPI is called *foreign indirect investment.*

[8] OECD, Benchmark Definition of FDI, Sections 1.4.11 and 2.3.2.29.

An investment barrier is any factor that regulates or restricts FDI in a nation-state or separate customs territory. Investment barriers include: (1) entry barriers to FDI and (2) post-entry barriers to FDI.

Regulating factors can be grouped into five subcategories:

- Tariff barriers
- Non-tariff barriers
- Other barriers to trade
- Entry barriers to FDI
- Post-entry barriers to FDI

Regulating factors are the most dominant factors that affect the conduct of international commerce, because: (1) they apply directly to the operations of entities engaged in the practice of international trade and/or FDI, and (2) they carry the force of national governmental authority. Trade barriers are discussed in Chapters 2, 3, 4, and in some parts of Chapter 6 (because some post-entry barriers to FDI act as barriers to trade). Investment barriers are discussed in Chapters 5 and 6.

1.2.2 Facilitating Factors

The primary factors that facilitate the conduct of international trade and FDI are the written agreements that are entered into by the governments of nation-states or by non-governmental organizations, which are referred to as *instruments*; and the functional and organizational entities that are created and controlled by the governments of nation-states or by non-governmental organizations, which are referred to as *mechanisms*.

Facilitating instruments include "The General Agreement on Tariffs and Trade," other World Trade Organization (WTO) instruments, and non-WTO global intergovernmental and non-governmental instruments; regional and bilateral preferential trade agreements (PTAs); and intergovernmental and non-governmental instruments that facilitate the formulation and dissemination of international standards, the harmonization of laws, and the settlement of disputes. Facilitating mechanisms include the WTO and other global intergovernmental and non-governmental organizations; regional trade blocks (RTBs)—which include free trade areas

(FTAs) and customs unions (CUs); and intergovernmental and nongovernmental organizations for international standards, the harmonization of laws, and the settlement of disputes.

Facilitating factors can be grouped into five subcategories:

- The GATT, the WTO, and other global instruments and mechanisms
- Regional and bilateral instruments and mechanisms
- International standards
- The harmonization of laws
- The settlement of disputes

These factors: (1) facilitate the reduction or elimination of barriers to trade and FDI; (2) facilitate the formulation and dissemination of international standards, the harmonization of laws, and the settlement of disputes; and (3) provide the framework and systems that facilitate the performance and operation of international trade and FDI. Facilitating factors are discussed in Chapters 7 through 12.

PART II
Regulating Factors

CHAPTER 2

Tariff Barriers

Contents

2.1 Terms and Definitions

Barriers to trade are divided into three categories: (1) Trade barriers that are tariffs, which are called *tariff barriers*; (2) *non-tariff barriers*; and (3) *other barriers to trade*.

Tariff barriers are discussed in this chapter. Non-tariff barriers are discussed in Chapter 3. Other barriers to trade are discussed in Chapter 4.[1]

2.1.1 Tariff Barriers

A tariff, trade tariff, or customs tariff: (1) is a set customs duty, (2) is on a published list, and (3) is applied to a category of products entering or leaving a country or separate customs territory. Tariffs can be applied to exports, but in practice almost all tariffs are on imports.[2]

2.1.2 Customs Duties

Duties are a form of tax. The meaning of the term *tax* is extremely broad: it can refer to any compulsory payment that is levied on individuals and/or entities, and is payable to a government. A duty is a tax that is levied on the sale or movement of a product or service. Duties that are applied to the sale or movement of a product within a country are called *excise duties*.[3]

The term *customs* refers to the government department that administers and collects duties levied on products entering or leaving a country. Duties that are applied to products entering or leaving a country are referred to broadly as *customs duties*.[4] Customs duties include tariffs, safeguards, anti-dumping duties, and countervailing duties.[5]

2.1.3 Customs Tariffs

The literal meaning of the word *tariff* is a list of fixed prices or fees that is made public.[6] In international trade, the term *tariff* or *customs*

---

[1] The distinction between non-tariff barriers and other barriers to trade is discussed in Chapter 4, Section 4.1.

[2] The reason most tariffs are on imports is discussed in Section 2.2.1.

[3] Excise duties are sometimes called *inland taxes*.

[4] Customs duties are sometimes called *border taxes*.

[5] Safeguards are discussed in Chapter 3, Section 3.3.3; anti-dumping duties are discussed in Chapter 4, Section 4.2; countervailing duties are discussed in Chapter 4, Section 4.3.4.

[6] The word tariff comes from the Italian *tariffa*: a list of prices or book of rates, which is derived from the Arabic *ta'rif*: to notify or announce.

tariff refers to a customs duty that is fixed, is listed on a customs tariff schedule, and applies to a particular *Harmonized System* (HS) product category[7] and to a product's country of origin.[8] Customs tariffs are classified as either *ad valorem tariffs* or *specific duty tariffs*. Some governments also use a combination of these two categories, which is called a *compound tariff*.

2.1.4   Ad Valorem Tariffs

Most trade tariffs are ad valorem.[9] An ad valorem tariff is based on a product's monetary value, is referred to as a *tariff rate*, and is expressed as a percentage.

The US: Cars

The trade tariff on cars is usually an ad valorem tariff. For example, the tariff rate on cars entering the United States is 2.5 percent. Based on this tariff rate, if the value of a car entering the US is $30,000, the tariff will be $750.

2.1.5   Specific Duty Tariffs

A *specific duty* tariff is an amount levied on each unit that is imported, or on each unit of quantity or weight that is imported. Specific duty tariffs are not expressed as a percentage, but as a monetary amount.

Indonesia: Rice

The tariff on the importation of rice into Indonesia is 450 rupiahs per kg. This is a specific duty tariff, because it is a monetary amount that applies to the quantity (by weight) of the rice being imported. Based on this tariff, if the amount of rice being imported is 1,000 kg, the tariff will be 450,000 rupiahs.

---

[7] HS product categories are discussed in Section 2.3.
[8] A product's country of origin is discussed in Section 2.4.
[9] The term *ad valorem* is Latin for *according to value.*

2.1.6   Tariff Rates and Amounts

The ad valorem tariff rate or specific duty tariff is governed by a product's category and country of origin. The tariff rate or amount of tariff on a product is not affected by the identity of the individual or entity that produced or exported the product.

The term *tariff rate* or *rate* is sometimes used as a general term when referring to either a tariff rate or a specific duty. For example, the "The General Agreement on Tariffs and Trade" (GATT)[10] uses the term *preferential rate of duty* when referring to a *preferential tariff rate* or a *preferential special duty*.[11]

2.2   The Purposes of Tariffs

The governments of nation-states use tariffs: (1) to protect the production, manufacture, and sale of domestic products, and to protect domestic companies, industries, and jobs; (2) to address balance of payments problems; (3) to generate revenue; and/or (4) to limit exports.

2.2.1   Protection

About 2,400 years ago, Socrates argued that the first role of government is to protect society. Most governmental leaders believe that every country has the right and the duty to protect its economic viability—and to protect the economic welfare of its citizens; and that they must, to this end, protect their country's companies, industries, and jobs by protecting the production, manufacture, distribution, and sale of domestically produced products.

When a government applies a tariff to an imported product, this adds to the cost of the product and increases the price at which the product must be sold to make a profit. By adding to the price at which imported products are sold, tariffs provide domestic producers and manufacturers

---

[10] All references to the GATT that do not specify a year are to GATT 1994 (which includes GATT 1947). This is discussed in Chapter 8, Section 8.4.3.2.
[11] GATT, Articles I, 4; II, 1, c; and V, 6. Preferential tariffs are discussed in Chapter 7, Section 7.1.6; and Chapter 9, Section 9.3.3.1.

with a competitive advantage. When a tariff is used primarily to protect domestic products—and/or to protect domestic companies, industries, or jobs—it is called a *protective tariff.*

Canada: Cheese

To protect the Canadian dairy and poultry industries, the government of Canada has established a *supply management* system, which controls the prices of milk, cheese, chicken, and eggs. The system includes three pillars: production controls, price controls, and import controls. The import controls include a 246 percent tariff on imported cheese.

The protection of domestic products, companies, industries, and/or jobs—and the need by some governments to manage their balance of payments—is why almost all tariffs are on imports.

2.2.2   Balance of Payments

Some countries have balance of payments problems, because the value of their imports far exceeds the value of their exports. To address these problems, some countries (and especially least developed countries[12]) use tariffs to reduce the number or amount of non-essential imports.[13]

2.2.3   Revenue Generation

For some countries, the primary reason for the use of tariffs has been to raise revenue.

The US: Revenue

The United States became a nation-state in 1789. Due to the cost of the war of independence between the American colonies

---

[12] The term *least developed countries* (LDC) is discussed in Chapter 7, Section 7.1.2.3; and refers to countries on the UNCTAD LDC list.

[13] For members of the WTO, this use of tariffs is governed by Article 9 of the 1994 Understanding on the Balance-Of-Payments Provisions of the General Agreement on Tariffs and Trade.

and England,[14] the US began with a large national debt. Also, it had no source of revenue with which to pay this debt or to pay for the operating and administrative costs of the government. To address these problems, the Congress of the United States passed the *Hamilton Tariff* of 1789, which levied tariffs on a list of imported products. In 1792, tariff revenues accounted for 100 percent of the US budget. Tariffs continued to be the largest single source of revenue for the US government until 1913, when it established an income tax. By 1944, revenues from tariffs had declined to about one percent of the US budget—and since then have continued to average about one percent.

Ukraine: Revenue

In 2014, in an attempt to reduce its budget deficit and satisfy foreign lender governments and the International Monetary Fund (IMF), the Supreme Council of Ukraine adopted measures that included additional tariffs on imports.

2.2.4 *Exports Limitation*

Most tariffs are on imports, but some tariffs are on exports. Some countries apply export duties for the purpose of limiting the exportation of their economic and/or economic development resources.

China: Aluminum, nickel, and copper

From 2005 through 2009, China applied duties on the export of aluminum, nickel, and copper—to conserve these national resources for use in China, and to discourage the use of China as the location for the processing of energy-intensive materials and products.

2.2.5 *Combinations*

Decisions by national governments related to the use of tariffs can be influenced by two or more of the above reasons.

---

[14] The American War of Independence, also called the *American Revolutionary War*, 1775 to 1783.

The US: Revenue and protection

In 1789, when the US Secretary of the Treasury, Alexander Hamilton, recommended the use of tariffs to raise revenue, he also argued that the application of tariffs would discourage imports and protect domestic industries.

2.3   Product Tariff Categories

In the conduct of international trade, the method used by governments to name and classify products—and to codify product tariff categories—is called the *Harmonized System* (HS). The HS is contained in the "International Convention on the Harmonized Commodity Description and Coding System" (the HS Convention),[15] which entered into force on January 1, 1988. The HS is revised every five years.

2.3.1   HS Codes

The principal functional element of the HS nomenclature and coding system is HS codes—which are also referred to as *HS classification codes*, *customs tariff codes*, *tariff codes*, and *tariff headings*. HS codes use more than 1,200 headings, which are grouped into 97 chapters and 21 sections.

In the following HS examples for categories of cars and rice, the first two digits are the chapter number, the first four digits are the heading number, all six digits are the HS code:

870323	Motor cars and other motor vehicles principally designed for the transport of persons (other than those of heading 87.02), including station wagons and racing cars. Other vehicles, with spark-ignition internal combustion reciprocating piston engine: Of a cylinder capacity exceeding 1,500 cc but not exceeding 3,000 cc
870324	Motor cars ... Of a cylinder capacity exceeding 3,000 cc
100610	Rice in the husk (paddy or rough)
100620	Husked (brown) rice

---

[15] The HS Convention was adopted by the contracting parties of the Customs Co-operation Council (CCC) in 1983, and entered into force in 1988. In 1994, the CCC changed its name to the World Customs Organization (WCO).

2.3.2   The Extension of HS Codes

Article 3 of the HS Convention says the six-digit numerical HS codes must not be modified, but a national government may modify the text to comply with domestic law. Countries may use an additional one or two pairs of digits (an additional two or four digits) to make product categories more specific, which results in 8- or 10-digit codes.[16] In some cases, the last pair of digits in a 10-digit code is used to facilitate the compilation of trade statistics.

> The US: HTSUS
>
> The Harmonized Tariff Schedule of the United States (HTSUS) came into effect in 1989.[17] HTSUS uses the HS codes and coding system; includes 1,700 headings, 99 chapters, and 22 sections; and uses 10-digit codes.

2.4   Country of Origin

In the conduct of international trade, the term *country of origin* is not a descriptor: it does not refer to the country or customs territory from where a product was exported. It is a technical term—that refers to the country or customs territory where the product was produced.

A product's country of origin affects its tariff rate and origin marking requirements (labeling), and can also affect other trade-related factors including quotas,[18] safeguard measures,[19] anti-dumping duties,[20] countervailing duties,[21] and preferential tariffs[22]—and the implementation of governmental procurement programs, trade embargos, and the generalized system of preferences (GSP).[23]

---

[16] Except that Saudi Arabia uses 12-digit codes.

[17] The HTSUS replaced the Tariff Schedules of the United States (TSUS).

[18] Quotas are discussed in Chapter 3, Section 3.3.2.

[19] Safeguards are discussed in Chapter 3, Section 3.3.3.

[20] Anti-dumping duties are discussed in Chapter 4, Section 4.2.

[21] Countervailing duties are discussed in Chapter 4, Section 4.3.4.

[22] Preferential tariffs are discussed in Section 2.1.6 of this chapter; Chapter 7, Section 7.1.6; and Chapter 9, Section 9.3.3.1.

[23] The GSP provides preferential tariffs on products from developing countries and territories.

Determining the country of origin of agricultural products (such as apples, rice, or cotton) is not difficult, because their country of origin is the country in which they are grown. It can, however, be difficult to determine the country of origin of manufactured products (such as shoes, clothes, cars, or computers)—which can include materials, parts, and components from different countries, and can include research, design, development, and manufacturing processes that occur in two or more countries.

2.4.1   Rules of Origin

The criteria used for determining a product's country of origin are called *rules of origin* (ROO). Rules of origin are divided into two categories: (1) preferential rules of origin and (2) non-preferential rules of origin. Preferential ROO apply to trade that occurs between countries that are members of the same free trade area (FTA).[24]

2.4.2   Non-Preferential Rules of Origin

Non-preferential ROO apply to trade that occurs between countries that are not members of the same free trade area. The governments of nation-states have created two global instruments[25] that contain non-preferential rules of origin: the "International Convention on the Simplification and Harmonization of Customs Procedures," which is called the *Kyoto Convention*,[26] and the "Agreement on Rules of Origin."[27] These instruments provide general standards and specific criteria for determining country of origin.

---

[24] Free trade areas and preferential ROO are discussed in Chapter 9, Section 9.3.

[25] Intergovernmental instruments are discussed in Chapter 7, Section 7.3.

[26] The Kyoto Convention was created by the Customs Co-operation Council (now the WCO), entered into force in 1974, and has been periodically revised. The Kyoto Convention is distinct from the Kyoto Protocol, which is the "United Nations Framework Convention on Climate Change."

[27] The "Agreement on Rules of Origin" was created during the Uruguay Round of multilateral trade negotiations (which is discussed in Chapter 8, Section 8.4.3.2), and entered into force in 1995. It is administered jointly by the WTO and the WCO.

2.4.3   Substantial Transformation

When the manufacture of a product includes processes in more than one country, the Kyoto Convention says its "origin should be determined according to the substantial transformation criterion."[28] The "Agreement on Rules of Origin" says the term *substantial transformation* refers to "the country where the last substantial transformation has been carried out."[29] There is, however, no generally agreed-upon method for determining what constitutes a substantial transformation, and the international harmonization[30] of this aspect of ROO has proven to be one of the most intractable issues in international trade.

Since 1995, the Harmonization Work Program (which was established by the "Agreement on Rules of Origin"), the WTO Committee on Rules of Origin (which comes under the WTO Council for Trade in Goods), and the Technical Committee on Rules of Origin (which is a committee of the WCO) have been working on the international harmonization of ROO. Most of this work has been on the codification of substantial transformation methods.

Most countries use one of three methods for determining substantial transformation:

1. The change-in-tariff-classification method defines a substantial transformation as a process that results in a change in two or more of the digits in a product's HS code.[31]
2. The value-added or ad valorem-percentage method says substantial transformation is a process that adds substantially to the value of a product.[32]
3. The special processing rule uses a list of special processing operations that are seen as effecting a substantial transformation of a product.

---

[28] The Kyoto Convention, Specific Annex K, Chapter 1, rules of origin, 2 and 3.
[29] The Agreement on Rules of Origin, Article 3(b).
[30] The harmonization of laws is discussed in Chapter 11, Section 11.2.3.2.
[31] HS codes are discussed in Section 2.3.1.
[32] The value-added method is discussed in Chapter 9, Section 9.3.3.4, in the ASEAN FTA example.

In some cases, countries modify one of these methods, combine elements from different methods, or use their own method.

The US: Change in name, character, or use

In the US, rules of origin are administered by the US Customs and Border Protection (CBP) of the US Department of Homeland Security. In cases that require the application of non-preferential ROO (that is, ROO that apply to trade that does not occur between members of a free trade area or customs union), the CBP uses the substantial transformation criterion on a case-by-case basis, "based on a change in name/character/use method (i.e., an article that consists in whole or in part of materials from more than one country is a product of the country in which it has been substantially transformed into a new and different article of commerce with a name, character, and use distinct from that of the article or articles from which it was so transformed)."[33]

2.5   The Decline in the Role of Tariff Barriers

In the past, tariffs were the most widely used factor in the regulation of international trade: governments could protect their countries' products, commercial entities, industries, and jobs by applying protective tariffs.

But the extraordinary effectiveness and success of the primary operational provisions contained in the GATT instrument,[34] together with the proliferation of preferential trade agreements and regional trade blocs,[35] have severely limited the ability of governments to use tariffs as a protective mechanism. This has resulted in an increase in the use and significance of non-tariff barriers and other barriers to trade.

---

[33] US Customs and Border Protection, US Rules of Origin.

[34] The GATT's primary operational provisions are discussed in Chapter 8, Section 8.4.

[35] PTAs are discussed in Chapter 7, Section 7.1.6; RTBs are discussed in Chapter 9, Section 9.2.

CHAPTER 3

Non-Tariff Barriers

Contents

3.1   Introduction

Trade barriers that are not tariffs are divided into two groups:
(1) *non-tariff barriers* (NTBs) and (2) *other barriers to trade*. Non-tariff
barriers are discussed in this chapter. Other barriers to trade are discussed
in Chapter 4. The reasons for the division between non-tariff barriers and
other barriers to trade are discussed in Chapter 4, Section 4.1.

Non-tariff barriers include three subcategories: (1) technical barriers
to trade, (2) non-technical barriers to trade, and (3) non-tariff barriers
on exports.

3.2   Technical Barriers to Trade

The term *technical barriers to trade* (TBT) refers to measures that restrict trade—that may be used by WTO members. These measures are covered in lists of *general exceptions* and *security exceptions* that are contained in Articles XX and XXI of the "The General Agreement on Tariffs and Trade" (GATT),[1] and in a list of *legitimate objectives* that are contained in the 1994 "Agreement on Technical Barriers to Trade" (TBT agreement).[2]

The most widely used technical barriers to trade are contained in Article XX.(b) of the GATT, which refers to measures that are "necessary to protect human, animal or plant life or health"; and in Article 2.2 of the TBT agreement, which states that the legitimate objectives of technical regulations include: "national security requirements; the prevention of deceptive practices; protection of human health or safety, animal or plant life or health, or the environment."[3]

3.2.1   Human Life and Health

Measures that protect human life, health, or safety include restrictions and regulations concerning the labeling requirements on food; restrictions on the importation of agricultural products that contain pesticide or chemical residues; restrictions on the importation of textiles and leather that have been treated with certain dyes; and safety certification requirements for electrical products.

The US: FDA and FSIS

The US Food and Drug Administration (FDA), which maintains inspection offices in the United States and seven other countries, is responsible for ensuring that the nation's food supply

---

[1] All references to the GATT that do not specify a year are to GATT 1994 (which includes GATT 1947). This is discussed in Chapter 8, Section 8.4.3.2.

[2] The TBT agreement is discussed in Chapter 10, Section 10.2.

[3] This list of *legitimate objectives* also appears at several other places in the TBT agreement.

for human and animal consumption is safe, sanitary, wholesome, and properly labeled.[4] The FDA's responsibilities cover all imported food except meat, poultry, and processed eggs, which come under the Food Safety and Inspection Service (FSIS) of the US Department of Agriculture (USDA). The FSIS is responsible for approving and auditing countries that may export meat, poultry, and processed eggs to the US, for determining that these countries have inspection programs that are equivalent to those in the US, and for administering the reinspection program in the US.[5]

3.2.2 Animal and Plant Life or Health

Measures that protect animal or plant life or health include restrictions and regulations relating to the health and protection of animals, plants, and the physical environment—such as requirements related to the recycling, reuse, biodegradability, and disposal of packaging.

The US: APHIS

The USDA's *Animal and Plant Health Inspection Service* (APHIS) is responsible for "keeping US agricultural industries free from pests and diseases ... "[6]

3.2.3 National Security and the Environment

Article XXI of the GATT contains several categories of security-related exceptions, which include fissionable materials and implements of war. Article 2.2 of the TBT agreement restates the list of general exceptions that are contained in Article XX.(b) of the GATT, and adds national security, the prevention of deceptive practices, and the environment.

---

[4] USFDA, Office of Global Operations.
[5] USDA, FSIS Office of International Affairs.
[6] USDA, Animal and Plant Health.

The US and the EU: Tariffs on steel and aluminum

In 2018, the US imposed a 25 percent tariff on steel, and a 10 percent tariff on aluminum, from the European Union (EU), on the grounds of national security.

China: Ban on the importation of solid waste

In 2020, China banned the importation of solid waste by revising its "Law on the Prevention and Control of Environmental Pollution by Solid Waste." Article 1 of the revised law states that it was "formulated for the purpose of protecting and improving the ecological environment, preventing and controlling environmental pollution by solid waste, safeguarding public health, maintaining ecological security, promoting the construction of ecological civilization, and promoting sustainable economic and social development."

3.2.4   The Misuse of Technical Barriers to Trade

As discussed in Chapter 2,[7] several factors have limited the ability of national governments to use tariff barriers to protect their countries' products, commercial entities, industries, and jobs. This has resulted in an increase in the use of non-tariff barriers and other barriers to trade, which has included an increase in the use of technical barriers to trade.

The first paragraph of Article XX of the GATT provides that technical barriers to trade must not be used as "a means of arbitrary or unjustifiable discrimination between countries" or as "a disguised restriction on international trade." Also, Article 2.2 of the TBT agreement provides that "members shall ensure that technical regulations are not prepared, adopted or applied with a view to or with the effect of creating unnecessary obstacles to international trade." These prohibitions notwithstanding, technical barriers to trade are frequently used by the governments of nation-states to protect their country's products, companies, industries, and/or jobs.

---

[7] Chapter 2, Section 2.5.

Germany: Electrical tools

In 2005, German Customs seized a large quantity of Chinese-made electrical tools (including those made by German companies ALDI and Bosch in China), on the grounds that these products contained a chemical carcinogen called PAH. The German government also started inspecting all Chinese-made electrical tools, and instructed retailers to not sell these products. These actions appear to have been an unjustifiable discrimination, and a disguised restriction on international trade, because: (1) at the time, neither Germany nor the European Union (EU) had standards relating to PAH in electrical tools; and (2) these actions were applied solely to products made in China.

The US and the EU: Tariffs on steel and aluminum

The application of tariffs on imports of steel and aluminum from the EU by the United States in 2018, on the grounds of national security, which is cited in the previous section, also appears to have been an unjustifiable discrimination and a disguised restriction on international trade. This is because: (1) steel and aluminum are not "fissionable materials" that are "necessary for the protection of ... essential security interests," which are TBTs under Article XXI.(b) of the GATT; and (2) the North Atlantic Treaty Organization (NATO) is the United States' primary national security alliance, and, in 2018, 21 members of the EU were members of NATO.

3.3   Non-Technical Barriers to Trade

Non-technical barriers can be divided into four groups: (1) administrative regulations, (2) quotas, (3) safeguards, and (4) systemic and structural factors.

3.3.1   Administrative Regulations

The purpose of trade-related administrative regulations is to facilitate the implementation of a country's trade policies and laws, and to regulate the conduct of its international trade. Some of the NTB administrative regulations discussed in this section are the same as, or similar to, some of the post-entry barriers to FDI that are discussed in Chapter 6.[8]

NTB administrative regulations can include:

- Restrictions on payments for imports;
- Local-content requirements;[9]
- Documentation requirements and customs, inspection, and certification procedures;
- Fees relating to administration, customs, inspection, and certification;
- Restrictions on imports related to production or manufacturing methods, such as restrictions on the importation of shrimp that were harvested using methods or equipment that threaten sea turtles, restrictions on the importation of products that include child-labor content, and restrictions on access to media and social media; and
- Market access barriers (including structural barriers).[10]

The regulation of access to foreign media and social media

The governments of some countries—which include, China, India, Iran, North Korea, Turkmenistan, and the United States—prevent or restrict access to Facebook, Google, TikTok, Twitter, WeChat, YouTube and/or other foreign media/social media platforms and applications, for a wide range of reasons that include cultural protection, national security, and preventing the incitement of ethnic violence. In September 2020, the US Department of Commerce banned the sale of the messaging apps WeChat and TikTok in the United States.[11]

---

[8] See Chapter 6, Section 6.4.

[9] Local content requirements are discussed in Chapter 6, Sections 6.2.2 and 6.3.1.1.

[10] In the field of international commerce, the term *market access* is defined by the WTO as "the conditions, tariff and non-tariff measures, agreed by members for the entry of specific goods into their markets." WTO Secretariat, Market access for goods.

[11] These bans were removed in June 2021.

Specific administrative regulations that can act as NTBs include:

- Administrative delays, including customs delays, and delays in anti-dumping and subsidy investigations;[12]
- Lack of clarity, consistency and/or transparency in regulations;[13]
- Inadequate protection for intellectual property rights;
- The absence of established procedures;[14] and
- The inconsistent and/or subjective application of laws and/or regulations.

The US: Country of origin rulings

In the US, delays in country of origin rulings by the CBP Office of Regulations and Rulings[15] can act as NTBs, because 65 percent of these rulings take up to three months to complete, and 35 percent take more than three months to complete.[16]

In practice, administrative regulations associated with technical barriers to trade can have indirect or secondary affects that act as non-technical barriers to trade.

China: CCC

The Compulsory Product Certification System, which is administered by the Certification and Accreditation Administration of China (CNCA), requires that all electrical products (and many other products) sold in China must carry the China Compulsory Certification Mark (CCC). The CCC requirement applies to products made in China and to imported products. In addition to testing products for safety and quality, the CNCA applies quality process standards[17] to the factories where products are

---

[12] Anti-dumping and subsidy investigations are discussed in Chapter 4, Sections 4.2.1 and 4.3.4.2.

[13] Transparency is discussed in Chapter 6, Section 6.4.2.

[14] The absence of established procedures is discussed in Chapter 6, Section 6.4.3.

[15] The administration of ROO in the US is discussed in Chapter 2, Section 2.4.3.

[16] U.S. Accountability Office. U.S. Customs Service.

[17] Quality process standards are discussed in Chapter 10, Section 10.3.2.

manufactured. Factories in foreign countries that make products for export to China must be inspected and certified for compliance with CCC standards. The purpose of the CCC requirement is to ensure the safety and quality of electrical and other products, and is, therefore, a technical barrier to trade (as defined in Article XX of the GATT). But because the costs and time delays associated with CCC inspection requirements for foreign manufacturers frequently result in expensive and complex inspection and certification procedures, these requirements can also act as a non-technical barrier to trade.

3.3.2 Quotas

A quota is a quantitative restriction on the number or amount of a product category—that may be imported or exported during a specific period.[18] Quotas allow a country to regulate the volume of, or tariff rate on, imports or exports of a specific product category from or to a specific country. Quotas are classified as either *absolute quotas* or *tariff rate quotas*.

3.3.2.1 Absolute Quotas

An absolute quota sets the maximum number or amount of a product category that may be imported from or exported to a country during a specific period.

The US and Japan: Cars

A series of agreements that were entered into by the governments of the United States and Japan between 1981 and 1994 applied quotas that restricted the number of Japanese cars that could be imported into the US each year.

China and the EU: Textiles

From 2005 through 2007, the government of China applied quantitative limits that restricted the amount of 10 categories of textiles that could be exported to the European Union.

---

[18] Article XI of the GATT provides for the "General Elimination of Quantitative Restrictions," but includes a list of exceptions.

3.3.2.2   Tariff-Rate Quotas

A tariff-rate quota (TRQ) sets the maximum number or amount of a product category that may be imported from a country at a preferential *in-quota* tariff (which can be as low as zero tariff) during a specific period. When the number or amount allowed by the quota has been reached, additional imports can continue at the non-preferential *over-quota* tariff.

The US and sub-Saharan Africa: TRQs

Under the Africa Growth and Opportunity Act of 2000, the United States maintains duty-free TRQs on a wide range of products, which include dairy, beef, cotton, peanuts, peanut butter and paste, tobacco, sugar, sugar containing products, textiles, and wearing apparel from about 40 eligible countries in sub-Saharan Africa.

Canada and the EU: Cheese

In 2013, Canada and the European Union entered into a "Comprehensive Economic and Trade Agreement" (CETA), which eliminated 98 percent of tariffs on Canadian products entering the EU, and gave products from the EU greater access to the commerce of Canada. One of the provisions of the CETA is that 29,000 million tonnes of cheese[19] from the EU may enter Canada annually at a zero in-quota tariff (that is, duty-free), after which EU cheese imports will be subject to an over-quota tariff of 246 percent.

Since 1995, there has been a sharp decline in the use of absolute quotas, and most quotas have been tariff-rate quotas. This shift in usage has been driven by the tariffication provisions contained in the "Agreement on Agriculture," which is one of the 60 agreements concluded in 1994 during the Uruguay Round of GATT negotiations.[20] The agreement's tariffication provisions prohibit the use of absolute quotas on agriculture trade between WTO member countries, but allow the use of tariff-rate quotas.

---

[19] This tonnage is about seven percent of Canada's annual domestic cheese market, which is about 420,000 tonnes.

[20] The Uruguay Round of GATT negotiations is discussed in Chapter 8, Section 8.4.3.2.

3.3.3   Safeguards

The term *safeguards* refers to functional mechanisms[21] for limiting imports that may be used by specific categories of countries, or by a country that needs to take an *emergency action*:

1. Article XII of the GATT, *Safeguard the Balance of Payments*, allows least developed countries that have balance of payment problems to use quotas to limit imports.[22]
2. Article XVIII of the GATT, *Governmental Assistance to Economic Development*, allows developing countries that are "in the early stages of development" to restrict the quantity or value of imports.
3. Article XIX of the GATT, Emergency Action on Imports of Particular Products, and the WTO "Safeguards Agreement" allow all WTO members to limit temporarily the importation of a product category if an increase in imports could cause serious injury to a domestic industry.

3.3.4   Systemic and Structural Factors

In some cases, a systemic or structural factor in an importing country's domestic commercial environment can act as a non-tariff barrier to trade. Some of these systemic or structural factors are governmental (such as the NTBs associated with administrative regulations, which are discussed in Section 3.3.1)—but some are non-governmental.

> The US and Japan: Cars
>
> In the 1980s, US car manufacturers argued that the principal reason they were unable to penetrate the Japanese car market was that, in Japan, the networks of new car distributors and dealers were owned and/or controlled by Japanese car manufacturers, and that this was a structural barrier to trade.

---

[21] Functional mechanisms are discussed in Chapter 7, Section 7.4.3.

[22] The term *least developed countries* (LDCs) is discussed in Chapter 7, Section 7.1.2.3. Because LDCs are a subcategory of developing countries, in this book references to developing countries include LDCs.

3.4   NTBs on Exports

Like tariffs, most non-tariff barriers apply to imports, but some NTBs apply to exports. NTBs that limit exports include: restrictions on exports on the grounds of national security; restrictions contained in voluntary export restraint agreements and orderly marketing agreements; duties intended to limit the export of national economic resources; and restrictions on the exportation of cultural property.

3.4.1   Exports and National Security

In some cases, a nation-state uses its national security to justify controlling or preventing the exportation of some product categories.

The US: DDTC and USML

"The US Government views the sale, export, and re-transfer of defense articles and defense services as an integral part of safeguarding US national security and furthering US foreign policy objectives. The Directorate of Defense Trade Controls (DDTC) … is charged with controlling the export and temporary import of defense articles and defense services covered by the United States Munitions List (USML)."[23]

In the past, the national security justification was used primarily to restrict the exportation of defense-related products and services—but is now also used to restrict the exportation of intellectual property and advanced technologies. The national security justification is used primarily by developed countries.

The US: Ban on the exportation of advanced computer chips to China

In September, 2022, the US National Security Advisor said that "technology export controls … can be a new strategic asset in the U.S. and allied toolkit to impose costs on adversaries, and

---

[23] US State Department, DDTC, Mission.

even over time degrade their battlefield capabilities."[24] In October 2022, the US Department of Commerce announced new rules that prohibit the exportation of "Certain Advanced Computing and Semiconductor Manufacturing Items"[25] from the US to listed entities and persons in China.

3.4.2 Export-Limiting Agreements

Voluntary export restraint agreements (VERs) and *orderly marketing agreements* (OMAs) are trade agreements between the governments of exporting countries and importing countries, that are intended to prevent a surge in exports that could injure an industry in the importing country. Exporting countries use these agreements to dissuade an importing country from applying trade barriers to their products.[26]

The US and Japan: Cars

The agreements between the US and Japan that are discussed in Section 3.3.2.1, which restricted the number of Japanese cars that could be imported annually into the United States, were voluntary export restraint agreements. In the 1981 agreement, the government of Japan agreed to limit the annual exportation of cars to the United States to 1.68 million. This limit was increased in subsequent agreements, and the agreements ended in 1994.

China and the EU: Textiles

In 2005, the government of China applied export duties to Chinese-made textiles being exported to the European Union.[27] China subsequently entered into an "orderly marketing agreement" with the EU, which included temporary duties and quotas.

---

[24] Remarks by the USNSA at the Special Competitive Studies Project. September 16, 2022.
[25] US Department of Commerce, Bureau of Industry and Security. October 13, 2022. Docket Nos. 220930-0204 and 220930-0205, US Federal Register.
[26] The terms *exporting country* and *importing country* are discussed in Chapter 7, Section 7.1.2.1.
[27] See Section 3.3.2.1.

If these duties had been permanent, they would have been tariffs. Because these duties were temporary, they were NTBs.

The Uruguay Round agreements,[28] which came into effect in 1995, have severely limited the use of voluntary export restraint agreements by WTO member countries.

3.4.3 The Exportation of Cultural Property

The term *cultural property* covers art and cultural artifacts, which can include a wide range of objects that are seen as having artistic, historical, or archaeological value. The two intergovernmental instruments that regulate international trade in cultural property are the UNESCO "Convention on the Means of Prohibiting and Preventing the Illicit Import, Export and Transfer of Ownership of Cultural Property," 1970, which has been ratified by 141 countries; and the UNIDROIT "Convention on Stolen or Illegally Exported Cultural Objects," 1995, which has been ratified by 51 countries. In addition to having ratified[29] one or both of these instruments, some countries have laws and/or regulations that restrict or prohibit the exportation of cultural property.

India: Cultural property

Section 11 of the Customs Act of 1962 authorizes the central government of India to take steps to prevent the illegal exportation of "national treasures of artistic, historic or archaeological value"; and, under Section 3.(3) of the Foreign Trade Development and Regulation Act of 1992, "antiquities are placed in the restricted category, therefore making their import or export deemed banned." In 1972, India ratified the UNESCO Convention and adopted the "Antiques and Art Treasures Act;" and in 1973 adopted the "Antiquities and Art Treasures Rules," which are administered by the Archaeological Survey of India, located in the Ministry of Culture. These rules specify the terms of ownership of

---

[28] The Uruguay Round agreements are discussed in Chapter 8, Section 8.4.3.2.
[29] Ratification is discussed in Chapter 7, Section 7.3.2.1.

a cultural property asset that is classified as a national treasure, and "limit the asset from being taken out of the country."[30]

The US: Cultural property

The United States ratified the UNESCO Convention in 1972, and in 1983 enacted the "Convention on Cultural Property Implementation Act" (CPIA). The CPIA includes definitions of cultural property, which are from Article 1 of the UNESCO Convention, and implements two of the Convention's provisions. With the exception of archaeological objects removed from federal or Native American lands, and protected wildlife—the US does not have any legislation or administrative regulations that restrict or prohibit the exportation of cultural property.[31]

[30] K. Naganand. 2020. *Art Law: Restrictions on the Export of Cultural Property and Artwork* (India), pp. 57–65.
[31] R.A. Darwell. 2020. *Art Law: Restrictions on the Export of Cultural Property and Artwork* (US), pp. 115–117.

CHAPTER 4

Other Barriers to Trade

Contents

4.1   Introduction

The anti-dumping duties, subsidies, countervailing duties, and the politicization of trade factors that are discussed in this chapter are all barriers to trade. It could be argued, therefore, that, because these factors are barriers to trade and are not tariffs, they are, by definition, non-tariff barriers. But the term *non-tariff barrier* is not a descriptor: it is a technical term that is applied to the three groups of barriers discussed in Chapter 3: technical barriers to trade, non-technical barriers to trade, and non-tariff barriers on exports. The technical term for trade barriers that are neither tariff barriers nor NTBs is *other barriers to trade*.

In addition to these nomenclature conventions, the trade barriers discussed in this chapter have operational characteristics that differentiate them from tariff barriers and NTBs. All of the tariff barriers and most of the NTBs discussed in Chapters 2 and 3 are entry barriers to trade: they restrict or regulate (and, in the case of NTBs, sometimes prevent) the entry of products into the commerce of an importing country. The anti-dumping duties and countervailing duties discussed in this chapter, however, are post-entry barriers to trade: they are applied to products after they have been introduced into the commerce of an importing country. The exception is domestic subsidies, which (like tariff barriers and NTBs) can act as entry barriers to trade, but subsidies differ from other entry trade barriers because they are governmental actions that can be seen as interfering with and contaminating the conditions that are necessary for the conduct of free trade, and can be seen, therefore, as a distortion of free trade.[1]

4.2   Anti-Dumping

Article VI of the "The General Agreement on Tariffs and Trade" (GATT),[2] defines the term *dumping* as when "products of one country are introduced into the commerce of another country at less than the normal value of the products."

The concept of dumping is unique to international commerce. When an individual or entity is engaged in the practice of domestic commerce

---

[1] The distorting effects of subsidies are discussed in Section 4.3.2.

[2] All references to the GATT that do not specify a year are to GATT 1994 (which includes GATT 1947). This is discussed in Chapter 8, Section 8.4.3.2.

in a free market economy, they may sell their products at whatever price they choose—including at a price that is below list price, or below the cost of production. In the conduct of international trade, however, Article VI of the GATT says that the practice of dumping "is to be condemned if it causes or threatens material injury to an established industry" in the country where it is introduced.

Article VI of the GATT also provides that if the government of an importing country determines that an imported product is being dumped, the government may impose a duty on the product to offset it being introduced at less than its normal value—and to achieve parity between its normal value and the price at which it is being introduced.

4.2.1   The Two-Part Test

Article VI of the GATT requires that if a government is conducting an investigation to determine if a product is being introduced into its country's commerce "at less than its normal value," it must use a two-part test: (1) less than normal value and (2) injury to a domestic industry.

> Note concerning US terminology: The government of the United States frequently uses the phrase less than fair value, instead of the phrase less than normal value, because the Tariff Act of 1930, and the US International Trade Commission Antidumping [sic] and Countervailing Duty Handbook, use the phrase less than fair value.

4.2.1.1   Part 1: Less Than Normal Value

The government of the importing country must determine if the product was imported "at less than its normal value."[3] There are three methods for determining normal value:

1. Domestic price. In most cases, the term *normal value* refers to the price at which a product is sold in the domestic market of the exporting country, or in the domestic market of a surrogate third country.[4]

---

[3] GATT, Article VI, 1.
[4] The surrogate third-country rule is discussed in Section 4.2.4.

If there is no "domestic price," because the product is not sold in the exporting country, normal value can be determined by using one of the following methods.

2. "The highest comparable price" at which the product is exported to a third country.

3. "The cost of production of the product in the country of origin[5] plus a reasonable addition for selling cost and profit."[6]

4.2.1.2   Part 2: Injury to a Domestic Industry

The government of the importing country must also determine if the imported product has caused or threatens to cause "material injury to an established industry … or materially retards the establishment of a domestic industry"[7] in the importing country.

4.2.1.3   The Two Necessary Conditions

For the government of the importing country to proceed with an anti-dumping investigation or to apply anti-dumping duties, both conditions of the two-part test must be present.

> The US and nine other countries: Pipes and tubes used in the oil industry
>
> In 2013, the US International Trade Commission (USITC) said it was pursuing an anti-dumping investigation because it had "determined that there is a reasonable indication that a US industry is materially injured by reason of imports of certain oil country tubular goods from India, [South] Korea, the Philippines, Saudi Arabia, Taiwan, Thailand, Turkey, Ukraine, and Vietnam that are allegedly sold in the United States at less than fair value."[8]

---

[5] The term *country of origin* is discussed in Chapter 2, Section 2.4.

[6] GATT, Article VI, 1(b)(ii).

[7] GATT, Article VI, 1.

[8] De Vera. n.d. "US Anti Dumping Case," The use of the term *fair value* (rather than *normal value*) by the US government is discussed in Section 4.2.1.

Australia and Greece: Currants

In 2014, the government of Australia announced that an earlier investigation had found Greek currants had been imported into Australia at "dumped prices"; that "the latest investigation has found dumping is still continuing"; that "the dumping of Greek currants into the Australian market resulted in injury to Australian manufacturers"—and that the government was applying anti-dumping duties of up to 8.1 percent on imported currants from Greece.[9]

The US and Japan and Spain: Methionine

In 2021, USITC determined that "a U.S. industry is materially injured by reason of imports of methionine from Japan and Spain that the U.S. Department of Commerce … has determined are sold in the United States at less than fair value."

If an anti-dumping investigation finds only one of the two necessary conditions is present, the importing country may not levy anti-dumping duties on the imported product.

The US, China, Germany, and Turkey: Wire rods

In 2005, the USITC investigated the importation of carbon and alloy steel wire rods from China, Germany, and Turkey. During the investigation, the steel manufacturers from these countries argued that: (1) imports of these products from China, Germany, and Turkey had declined in the first nine months of 2005, (2) demand for these products in the US exceeded supply, and (3) the profits of US wire rod makers had declined slightly in 2005, but were still higher than the average for previous years. The USITC found that the products covered in this investigation had been imported at less than normal value—but also found the importation of these products had not caused or threatened to cause material injury to US manufacturers. Because only one of the two necessary conditions was present, the US government did not apply anti-dumping duties.

---

[9] Baldwin. n.d. "Anti-dumping Ruling."

4.2.2   Anti-Dumping Duties

Article VI, 2. of the GATT uses the term *anti-dumping duty* (ADD) when referring to the duty that the government of an importing country may apply to an import that it has determined has been dumped. An anti-dumping duty is not a tariff; it is not a set duty on a published list that is applied to a category of products—but is a specific duty that is applied to a specific product, that is imported from a specific country, by a specific company, at a specific price.

4.2.2.1   The Level of Anti-Dumping Duties

The purpose of anti-dumping duties is not punitive, but is to offset the less than normal value at which a product is being "introduced into the commerce" of the importing country.

The difference between a product's normal value and the price at which it is being introduced is called the *margin of dumping*. Because the purpose of an anti-dumping duty is to achieve parity between a product's normal value and the price at which it is being introduced, the amount of an ADD applied by the government of an importing country may not exceed the margin of dumping.

> The EU, Argentina, and Indonesia: Biodiesel
>
> In 2013, the European Union imposed anti-dumping duties on imports of biodiesel[10] from Argentina and Indonesia. The European Commission said, "the bio-diesel anti-dumping duties do not constitute a punishment, but are imposed strictly to prevent further injury to the EU industry"; and that the duties will be imposed "at the level of the injury margin," which for Argentina is between 22 and 25.7 percent, and for Indonesia is between 8.8 and 20.5 percent.[11]

---

[10] Biodiesel is produced from soya beans and soybean oil in Argentina, and from palm oil in Indonesia.

[11] Giannoulis. n.d. "EU Imposes Anti-Dumping Duties."

4.2.2.2   Ad Valorem and Specific Anti-Dumping Duties

An anti-dumping duty can be either an ad valorem duty or a specific duty.[12] These two forms of ADD are similar to the ad valorem tariffs and specific duty tariffs discussed in Chapter 2, Sections 2.1.4 and 2.1.5. An ad valorem ADD is based on a product's monetary value, and is expressed as a percentage. A *specific* ADD is levied on each unit, or on each unit of quantity or weight—and is expressed not as a percentage, but as a monetary amount.

> The EU, Argentina, and Indonesia: Biodiesel
> In the previous example, the duties on biodiesel of between 22 and 25.7 percent for Argentina, and between 8.8 and 20.5 percent for Indonesia, are ad valorem ADDs, because these ADDs: (1) were based on the product's monetary value, and (2) were expressed as a percentage.

> Mexico and China: Seamless steel pipe
> In 2014, Mexico imposed anti-dumping duties of $1,568.92 per metric tonne on imports of some categories of seamless steel pipe from China. These were specific ADDs, because these ADDs: (1) were levied on each unit of weight (on each metric tonne), and (2) were expressed as a monetary amount ($1,568.92).

4.2.3   Espousal of Anti-Dumping Claims

If a company's products are the object of an anti-dumping investigation, the company may request its home-country government[13] to espouse its claim with the government of the importing country, or, following the imposition of anti-dumping duties, to bring a complaint to the WTO Dispute Settlement Body (DSB).[14]

---

[12] Ad valorem tariffs and specific duty tariffs are discussed in Chapter 2, Sections 2.1.4 and 2.1.5.

[13] The term *home country* is discussed in Chapter 7, Section 7.1.2.1.

[14] The WTO Dispute Settlement Body is discussed in Chapter 12, Section 12.4.

4.2.3.1   With the Government of an Importing Country

Trade disputes between the government of an importing country and a foreign company[15] can be highly problematic for the company, because the legal playing fields are not level.[16] When the company's claim is espoused by its home-country government, this helps to level the playing fields and increase the possibility of a mutually acceptable outcome.

Saudi Arabia and India: Petrochemicals

In January 2014, Saudi Arabia's minister for commerce and industry, Tawfiq Al-Rabiah, said the government of India had dropped its anti-dumping investigation against Saudi-based Chemanol Company (the kingdom's only exporter of pentaerythritol)—and that during the investigation: Chemanol was able to show it was not importing the product at less than normal value; the kingdom had raised the issue at meetings of the Saudi-Indian Joint Commission; the Saudi Embassy in New Delhi had coordinated with Indian authorities; and that the ministry's efforts, in coordination with Chemanol, had "helped in ending the investigation launched by the Indian authorities."[17]

4.2.3.2   With the WTO Dispute Settlement Body

If an anti-dumping dispute between a foreign company and the government of an importing country cannot be resolved, the company may choose to have the dispute taken to the WTO DSB.[18] In these situations, the dispute can proceed only if the company's home-country government agrees to espouse the company's claim, because the WTO is an intergovernmental organization—and only countries and separate customs territories have standing to bring a complaint to the WTO DSB.

---

[15] These disputes are called disputes between nation-states and nationals of other nation-states, and are discussed in Chapter 12, Section 12.2.5.

[16] This aspect of trade disputes is discussed in Chapter 12, Section 12.2.1.

[17] Ghafour. n.d. "KSA Wins Case."

[18] The use of the DSB is discussed in Chapter 12, Section 12.4.

The EU and Argentina: Biodiesel

Following the imposition of anti-dumping duties by the European Union on biodiesel imports from Argentina and Indonesia in 2013, which is discussed in Sections 4.2.2 and 4.2.2.2, the government of Argentina espoused the claim on behalf of the three Argentine companies and filed a complaint against the EU with the WTO Dispute Settlement Body.

4.2.4   The Anti-Dumping Surrogate Third-Country Rule

Article VI of the GATT provides that, when determining normal value, "due allowance shall be made in each case for … differences affecting price comparability." Because of this provision, if the exporting country is not a market economy, the government of the importing country may use a surrogate third country when determining normal value. In these cases, normal value refers to the price at which similar products are sold in the domestic market of the surrogate third country.

China and the EU: CD and DVD products

When the government of China negotiated the terms of its accession to membership in the WTO, which came into effect in 2001, China agreed to allow WTO members to treat it as a non-market economy in anti-dumping cases until 2016. In 2005, the European Union held anti-dumping investigations into the importation of CD-R and DVD+/-R products from the mainland of China. When determining if these products were being imported at less than normal value, the EU used Malaysia as the surrogate third country in the CD-R investigation, and used Taiwan as the surrogate third country in the DVD+/-R investigation.

4.3   Subsidies and Countervailing Duties

The 1994 WTO "Agreement on Subsidies and Countervailing Measures" (SCM)[19] defines a subsidy as a "financial contribution by a government

---

[19] The SCM is one of the agreements concluded during the Uruguay Round of multilateral trade negotiations. The Uruguay Round is discussed in Chapter 8, Section 8.4.3.2.

or any public body within the territory of a Member"[20] if the financial contribution benefits "an enterprise or industry or group of enterprises or industries ... within the jurisdiction of the granting authority ...."[21] In this SCM definition, a financial contribution by a government includes a financial contribution by a state or municipal government.[22]

The WTO's 2006 "World Trade Report" says the term *subsidy*, as defined in the SCM, applies only to financial contributions that are made to enterprises or industries located within "a WTO member's own territory."[23] This makes an important distinction between subsidies and anti-dumping provisions,[24] which are actions by the government of an importing country.

4.3.1   Types of Subsidies

The types of financial contributions covered by the SCM definition include:

- The direct transfer of funds, such as grants, loans, and equity infusions;
- The potential direct transfer of funds, such as loan guarantees;
- Government revenue "foregone or not collected," such as tax exemptions and fiscal incentives, which are commonly called *tax breaks*;
- Goods and services provided by the government, other than general infrastructure;[25]
- The governmental purchase of products; and
- Any income or price support that operates directly or indirectly to increase exports of any product from, or reduce imports into, the territory of the granting authority.

---

[20] SCM, Article 1.1(a)(1).
[21] SCM, Article 2.1.
[22] See the Airbus and Boeing example, in Section 4.3.3.2.
[23] World Trade Report. 2006. II.B.3, 54.
[24] Anti-dumping provisions are discussed in Section 4.2.
[25] The general infrastructure exception is discussed in Section 4.3.3.3, Item 1.

The SCM definition includes financial contributions covered by any of these categories, even if the payment has been made "to a funding mechanism" or through "a private body."[26] In practice, the provisions contained in the SCM categories are seen as covering a wide range of governmental financial contributions or other governmental actions that support domestic producers, which include:

- Governmental assistance programs, such as support programs that provide farmers or manufacturers with tax exemptions and tax credits, or with low-interest or interest-free loans;
- Governmental measures to support or protect domestic industries, including government sponsored "buy-national" programs;
- Governmental procurement policies (such as preference for domestic products when procuring defense-related products, and in other government purchasing), and government monopolies; and
- Governmental support for the development of new products, or for the establishment of new industries or new industry segments.

4.3.2   The Distorting Effects of Subsidies

The term *distortion of free trade* refers to the effects of governmental actions that interfere with and contaminate the conditions that are necessary for the conduct of free trade. Most subsidies are made by governments as part of their domestic economic development policies and programs, and their purpose is not primarily to affect trade. But their intended purpose notwithstanding, the financial subsidies paid to farmers and manufacturers have the effect of artificially reducing production costs, which can have a distorting effect on free trade by allowing these producers: (1) to sell their products domestically at artificially low prices, which can make it more difficult for imported products to compete with the domestically produced products, and (2) to export their products at artificially low prices.

---

[26] SCM, Article 1.1(a)(1)(iv).

4.3.3   *Prohibited, Actionable, and Allowed Subsidies*

Financial contributions by governments and public bodies are classified as prohibited subsidies, actionable subsidies, or allowed subsidies.

4.3.3.1   Prohibited Subsidies

In Part II: Prohibited Subsidies, Article 3, the SCM says subsidies are prohibited if they are:

1. "Contingent … upon export performance."[27] Subsidies in this group, which are commonly referred to as *export subsidies*, are listed in an annex to the SCM.[28]
2. "Contingent … upon the use of domestic over imported goods."[29] Subsidies in this group are sometimes referred to as *local-content subsidies*.

4.3.3.2   Actionable Subsidies

In Part III: Actionable Subsidies, Article 5, the SCM says WTO members should not use any subsidy that will cause "adverse effects" to another WTO member. These adverse effects are divided into two types:

1. "Injury to the domestic industry of another Member"[30]
   When applied to subsidies, the injury to a domestic industry criterion is similar to the application of this criterion in anti-dumping cases.
2. "Serious prejudice to the interests of another Member"[31]
   The term *serious prejudice*, as defined in Article 6 of the SCM, refers to subsidies that can result in the distortion of free trade,[32] and

---

[27] SCM, Article 3.1.1.
[28] This prohibition exempts subsidies that are "provided in the Agreement on Agriculture."
[29] SCM, Article 3.1.2.
[30] SCM, Article 5.1.
[31] SCM, Article 5.3.
[32] The distortion of free trade is discussed in Section 4.3.2.

include subsidies that exceed 5 percent of a product's value or that cover operating losses or the forgiveness of debt—if the effect of the subsidy (1) displaces or impedes imports, (2) causes significant price suppression in the domestic market, or (3) increases the country's "world market share" of a product.[33]

The provisions contained in Part III of the SCM are called *actionable subsidies*, because they can be the object of a countervailing action by another member, or can be the grounds for a complaint to an intergovernmental dispute settlement mechanism.[34]

The US and the EU: Airbus and Boeing

In 2004, the United States government filed a complaint with the WTO Dispute Settlement Body (WTO DSB),[35] which asserted that Airbus had received subsidies from the European Community,[36] the European Union, and the governments of Germany, France, the United Kingdom (UK), and Spain. The complaint said the subsidies were in the form of loans, grants, equity, and debt forgiveness; were related to the development of large civil aircraft; and totaled more than $22 billion. The EU responded the same year, by filing a complaint with the WTO DSB, which asserted that Boeing had received subsidies from departments and agencies of the United States government;[37] from the state governments of Kansas, Illinois, and Washington; and from municipal governments in these states. The complaint said the subsidies were in the form of tax and non-tax incentives, funding, support, and tax relief; and totaled more than $24 billion.

This dispute between the US and the EU over subsidies to Airbus and Boeing, and subsequent claims, counterclaims, appeals,

---

[33] These factors are discussed in SCM, Article 6.

[34] Intergovernmental dispute settlement mechanisms are discussed in Chapter 12, Section 12.2.3.

[35] WTO Dispute Settlement Body is discussed in Chapter 12, Section 12.4.

[36] The European Community is an organizational element of the European Union.

[37] These included the Department of Defense, the Department of Commerce, the Department of Labor, and the National Aeronautics and Space Administration.

and the imposition of related duties continued for 17 years. For example, in 2013, Boeing announced it would build its new 777X aircraft in Washington state, after the state legislature approved $8.7 billion in new tax breaks to the aerospace industry. In 2014, the EU launched a separate complaint with the WTO DSB, claiming these tax breaks by Washington state were actionable subsidies; and in 2016, the WTO ruled in favor of the EU.

In 2019, the WTO DSB (in separate decisions) found that Washington state was still providing subsidies in the form of tax breaks to Boeing; found that the EU was continuing to subsidize Airbus; and allowed the US to impose $7.5 billion in countervailing duties[38] and cross-retaliation duties[39] on EU imports. In 2019, the US imposed 10 percent countervailing duties on the importation of most Airbus planes, and 25 percent in cross-retaliation duties on non-aircraft products (which included cheese, olives, and single-malt whisky) from the EU. In 2020, the US increased the duties on aircraft imported from the EU to 15 percent. The same year, Washington state withdrew the tax breaks that benefited Boeing, which, since 2004, had been a central element of the EU's complaints.

In June 2021, the US and the EU reached an agreement to discontinue their dispute over subsidies to Airbus and Boeing, and suspended related countervailing duties (subject to the other party complying with the terms of the agreement).

4.3.3.3   Allowed Subsidies

There are three groups of subsidies that are allowed:

1. Contributions that fall outside the SCM definition[40]
   Allowed subsidies include contributions that are related to the development or improvement of general infrastructure (including roads,

---

[38] Countervailing duties are discussed in Section 4.3.4.
[39] Cross-retaliation duties are discussed in Section 4.3.4.3.
[40] The SCM definition of a subsidy is provided in Section 4.2.

port facilities, water and gas reticulation, and electricity grids), to non-company-specific and non-industry-specific tax incentives, and to other contributions that do not benefit "an enterprise or industry or group of enterprises or industries."[41]

2. "Non-actionable subsidies"

Part IV: Non-actionable subsidies, Article 8, of the SCM lists some exceptions to the subsidies in the actionable category, which are called *non-actionable subsidies*. These exceptions include "assistance for research activities conducted by firms or by higher education or research establishments,"[42] "assistance to disadvantaged regions within the territory of a Member,"[43] and "assistance to promote adaptation of existing facilities to new environmental requirements."[44] Each of these exceptions is narrowly defined—and is subject to limitations and conditions.

3. Developing countries

Part VIII: Developing Country Members, Article 27, of the SCM says that because "subsidies may play an important role in economic development programs of developing country Members," the prohibition on the use of subsidies shall not apply to least developed countries[45] that are members of the WTO, and for a limited time to other developing country members.

An allowed subsidy cannot be the object of a countervailing action by another member, and cannot be the grounds for a complaint by another member to an intergovernmental dispute settlement mechanism.

The US and the EU: Airbus and Boeing

A large part of the work done by the WTO DSB panels and Appellate Body[46] when they were deciding the Airbus and

---

[41] SCM, Article 2.1.

[42] SCM, Article 8.2.1.

[43] SCM, Article 8.2.2.

[44] SCM, Article 8.2.3.

[45] Least developed countries are discussed in Chapter 7, Section 7.1.2.3.

[46] WTO DSB panels and the WTO Appellate Body are discussed in Chapter 12, Section 12.4.2.

Boeing complaints filed by the US and the EU in 2004,[47] was to establish the facts and decide issues of law to determine if each of the alleged subsidies was actionable or non-actionable.[48] These complaints were the largest cases to have been handled by the WTO DSB, and this work took more than six years to complete.[49] The 2011 and 2012 Appellate Body reports found that, in both cases, some of the alleged subsidies were actionable and some were non-actionable. The reports also found that the actionable subsidies had, inter alia, caused serious prejudice[50] to the US and the EU, and had resulted in significant losses in sales by both Airbus and Boeing.

4.3.4   Countervailing Duties

In Part V: Countervailing Measures, Article 10, the SCM defines the term *countervailing duty* as "a special duty levied for the purpose of offsetting any subsidy bestowed directly or indirectly upon the manufacture, production or export of any merchandise, as provided for in paragraph 3 of Article VI of GATT 1994." In most cases,[51] a countervailing duty (CVD) is a trade remedy that is applied to products made by a specific company that has benefited from specific governmental financial contributions in a specific exporting country.

The US and the EU: Airbus and Boeing

Following the determinations by the WTO DSB in 2011 and 2012, the US government requested authorization from the DSB to impose CVDs of $12 billion annually on Airbus; the EU requested authorization from the DSB to impose CVDs of $7 billion to $10 billion annually on Boeing.

---

[47] These complaints are discussed in Section 4.3.3.2.

[48] The roles of panels and the Appellate Body at the WTO DSB are discussed in Chapter 12, Section 12.4.2.

[49] Article 12.8 of the 1994 Understanding provides that "the period in which the panel shall conduct its examination ... shall, as a general rule, not exceed six months." The 1994 Understanding is discussed in Chapter 12, Section 12.4.

[50] "Serious prejudice to the interests of another Member" is discussed in Section 4.3.3.2, Item 2.

[51] An exception is cross-retaliation duties, which are discussed in Section 4.3.4.3.

4.3.4.1 The Purpose and Level of CVDs

The purpose of a countervailing duty is to offset and nullify the financial benefit that has been contributed by the government (or by governments and/or by a public body) in an exporting country—by adding to the price at which the subsidized product is sold in the importing country. As with anti-dumping duties,[52] CVDs are not intended to be punitive—but are intended only to offset and nullify the benefit conferred by a subsidy. Article 19.4 of the SCM says a countervailing duty on an imported product must not exceed "the amount of the subsidy found to exist."

4.3.4.2 The Two-Part Test

Before applying countervailing duties, a governmental investigation must determine: (1) that an imported product has benefited from a subsidy, and (2) that this benefit has caused "adverse effects" to another WTO member. Adverse effects can be either "injury to the domestic industry of another Member" or "serious prejudice to the interests of another Member."[53] In some cases, a governmental investigation determines that a product has benefited from a subsidy, but determines that the subsidy has not caused adverse effects.

> The US and China, Ecuador, India, Malaysia, and Vietnam: Shrimp
>
> In August 2013, in response to a petition filed by the US Coalition of Gulf Shrimp Industries, the US Department of Commerce announced that imports of shrimp from China, Ecuador, India, Malaysia, and Vietnam had benefited from governmental subsidies in their countries of origin, and that the department was imposing CVDs on these imports of between 7.8 and 54.5 percent—subject to a review by the US International Trade Commission.
>
> In September 2013, the USITC announced it was rescinding the decision by the Department of Commerce, because

---

[52] The purpose and level of anti-dumping duties is discussed in Section 4.2.2.
[53] This two-part test is similar to the two-part test used in anti-dumping investigations, which is discussed in Section 4.2.1.

"a US industry is neither materially injured nor threatened with material injury by reason of imports of frozen warm water shrimp from China, Ecuador, India, Malaysia, and Vietnam that the US Department of Commerce has determined are subsidized."[54] In this case, the USITC did not disagree with the department's finding that the imports were subsidized—but disallowed the imposition of the CVDs based solely on the absence of adverse effects.

4.3.4.3   Cross-Retaliation Duties

Most countervailing duties are applied to products that have benefited from subsidies. In some cases, however, an importing country applies CVDs to products that have not benefited from a subsidy—to countervail against the effects of subsidies on another product. These CVDs are referred to as *cross-retaliation duties*.

The US and Brazil: Cotton

In 2002, the government of Brazil brought a complaint to the WTO Dispute Settlement Body against the US, for the annual payment of more than three billion dollars in subsidies to cotton farmers. In 2004, a WTO arbitration panel found the US subsidies had injured Brazil. In 2007, 2008, and 2009, the WTO authorized Brazil to apply several countervailing remedies, including cross-retaliation duties, against a wide range of products (including intellectual property imports) from the US.

The US and the EU: Airbus and Boeing

As discussed in the Airbus and Boeing example in Section 4.3.3.2, following the 2019 decision by the WTO DSB, which allowed the US to impose cross-retaliation duties on EU imports, the US imposed 25 percent cross-retaliation duties on cheese, olives, single-malt whisky, and other non-aircraft products from the EU.

---

[54] USITC, *Frozen Warmwater Shrimp*. In this announcement, the USITC said imports take up 35.7 percent of the US industry, which includes 48 producers and 2,050 workers.

4.4   The Politicization of Trade Barriers

The extraordinary success of the provisions contained in the GATT instrument, and their implementation by the de facto GATT organization and the WTO,[55] has made it difficult for national governments to politicize the use of tariffs. But the latitude provided by the general exceptions contained in Article XX of the GATT,[56] and by the rules contained in the WTO's "Agreement on Technical Barriers to Trade" (TBT agreement),[57] allow for the politicization of NTBs and other trade barriers.

Germany: Electrical tools

The German government's seizure of a large quantity of Chinese-made electrical tools (which is discussed in Chapter 3, Section 3.2.4), on the grounds that these products contained a chemical carcinogen called PAH, appear to have been influenced by domestic political factors.

The US: Steel and aluminum

In 2002, the US government applied safeguard duties of between 8 and 30 percent to some categories of steel entering the US.[58] The application of these duties appears to have been politically motivated because, during the 2000 presidential campaign, George W. Bush had promised steel workers in West Virginia that, if elected, he would apply these duties.

In 2018, the US imposed a 25 percent tariff on steel, and a 10 percent tariff on aluminum, from the EU, on the grounds of

---

[55] The success of these provisions is discussed in Chapter 8, Section 8.4.4.

[56] Article XX of the GATT and technical barriers to trade are discussed in Chapter 3, Section 3.2.

[57] The TBT agreement is discussed in Chapter 8, Sections 8.4.3.2 and 8.4.3.3; and Chapter 10, Section 10.2.

[58] Canada and Mexico were exempted from these duties. The EU, followed by Japan, South Korea, China, Taiwan, Switzerland, and Brazil filed a complaint with the WTO DSB, which, in November 2003, decided against the US and authorized more than $2 billion in sanctions if the duties were not removed. The duties were removed in December 2003.

national security.[59] Given that, at the time, the US and 21 members of the EU were members of the North Atlantic Treaty Organization (NATO), these actions appear to have been influenced by domestic political factors.

4.4.1 Political Risk

When an entity engaged in the practice of international trade and/or FDI is exposed to the possibility of adverse effects that could result from the politicization of a government's regulatory authority, this exposure is called *political risk*.

The term *political risk* can apply to an exposure to an action by a government's legislative, executive, or judicial branch (or an action by a combination of two or all three of these branches of a government); and can apply to an exposure to the politicized treatment of an enterprise, its shareholders, its assets—and/or its trade and/or FDI operations. Because the *risk* part of the term refers to an exposure, the term *political risk* refers literally to an exposure to the possibility of an adverse effect that could result from politicization. But the term *political risk* is also used when referring to a politicized action that has been taken by a government.

Political risk exposures and their operational effects can range in severity from delays in an enterprise receiving an administrative approval or authorization (until a government official has received a facilitating or expediting payment[60]) or the temporary imposition of increased tariffs or safeguard duties to protect a politically sensitive industry—which can increase the difficulty and costs associated with the conduct of international trade; to a government's adoption and application of a law and/or administrative regulations that discriminates against trade or FDI in a politically sensitive industry—or against trade or FDI by a specific foreign enterprise in a politically sensitive industry, the imposition of governmental regulatory controls and requirements that result in industry-specific or

---

[59] This is discussed in Chapter 3, Section 3.2.4.

[60] For the use of facilitating and expediting payments, see US Justice Department, Foreign Corrupt Practices Act. §78dd-3(b).

company-specific creeping expropriation, or governmental expropriation or nationalization of a foreign-funded enterprise or its assets.

Political risk exposures can be grouped into three specificities: (1) industry-specific political risk, (2) home-country-specific political risk, and (3) company-specific political risk. These types of political risk are discussed in Chapter 5, Section 5.6.2, and Chapter 6, Section 6.5.5.

4.4.2   Frequency and Severity

The highest number of politicized actions by governments are those that affect international trade. But the adverse effects of trade-related political risks are, in most cases, less severe than the adverse effects of the politicization of post-entry barriers to FDI.[61]

The German Electrical Tool and the US Steel and aluminum examples in Section 4.4 affected entities engaged in the conduct of international trade, but the severity of these exposures was relatively low. These governmental actions increased significantly the difficulty and costs associated with the conduct of international trade—but neither of these situations resulted in the loss of control of an entity's international trade operations, nor the loss of control or ownership of an entity's foreign direct investment.[62]

---

[61] The politicization of entry barriers to FDI is discussed in Chapter 5, Section 5.6. The politicization of post-entry barriers to FDI is discussed in Chapter 6, Section 6.5.

[62] Political risk-related loss of control or ownership is discussed in Chapter 6, Sections 6.5.2.2, 6.5.3, and 6.5.4.

CHAPTER 5

Entry Barriers to FDI

Contents

5.1   Introduction

Barriers to FDI can be divided into two groups: (1) entry barriers to FDI and (2) post-entry barriers to FDI. Entry barriers to FDI are discussed in this chapter; post-entry barriers to FDI are discussed in Chapter 6. The term *entry barriers to FDI* refers to barriers that restrict, regulate, or prohibit the entry of FDI into the commerce of a host country.[1]

5.2   Foreign Direct Investment

The term *foreign direct investment* refers to investment that is made in a nation-state by an individual or entity that is a national of another nation-state.[2] The term also includes investment by an individual or entity that is a national of the nation-state that is the location of the investment, but is a resident of a separate customs territory.[3]

There is no generally accepted definition of foreign direct investment, because the criteria that define FDI are set by the government of each host country.[4] There is, however, a widely used definition that was developed by the Organization of Economic Cooperation and Development (OECD).[5]

5.2.1   The OECD Benchmark

The OECD benchmark defines FDI as "a category of cross-border investment" that is made for the purpose of "establishing a lasting interest in an enterprise."[6]

---

[1] The term *host country* is discussed in Chapter 7, Section 7.1.2.1.
[2] Corporate nationality is discussed in Chapter 7, Section 7.1.4.
[3] Separate customs territories are discussed in Chapter 7, Section 7.1.3.
[4] The term *host country* is discussed in Chapter 7, Section 7.1.2.1.
[5] The OECD, which was established in 1961, is an intergovernmental organization that has 38 member countries. Until recently, the members of the OECD were all economically developed countries, but now include developing countries.
[6] All quotations in Sections 5.2.1 and 5.2.1.1 are from OECD, *Benchmark Definition of FDI*, Section 1.4.11 or 2.3.2.29.

The motivation of the direct investor is a strategic long-term relationship with the direct investment enterprise to ensure a significant degree of influence by the direct investor in the management of the direct investment enterprise.

The OECD benchmark also says, "the direct investor owns at least 10 percent of the voting power of the direct investment enterprise." But the principal criteria contained in the OECD benchmark are qualitative rather than quantitative: they address the investor's purpose and motivation.

The main motivation of the direct investor is to exert some degree of influence over the management of its direct investment enterprise, whether or not this entails exercising a controlling interest. The motivation to significantly influence or control an enterprise is the underlying factor that differentiates direct investment from cross-border portfolio investments.

5.2.1.1   Foreign Portfolio Investment

Foreign portfolio investment (FPI), which the OECD benchmark calls *cross-border portfolio investment* (and is sometimes called *foreign indirect investment*), is discussed in Chapter 1, Section 1.1.3. When an investor is engaged in FPI, their focus "is mostly on earnings resulting from the acquisition and sales of shares and other securities without expecting to control or influence the management of the assets underlying these investments."

Because FPI does not provide foreign investors with "some degree of influence over the management of its direct investment enterprise," and does not provide them with a significant degree of influence or control over the operations of an entity in which they have made a portfolio investment, FPI cannot be used as part of a foreign investor's commercial operations.

5.2.1.2   The Focus on FDI

Investment barriers that apply to FDI do not apply to FPI, and references to foreign investment in WTO instruments apply only to FDI. For example, references to investment in the 1994 "Agreement on Trade-Related Investment Measures" (TRIMs),[7] which is part of the body of WTO instruments,[8] refer only to FDI, and not to FPI. For these reasons, and the reasons covered in Chapter 1, Section 1.1.3, the discussion of foreign investment in this book is focused solely on FDI.

5.2.2   FDI Process Options

The processes used to engage in FDI can be classified as either build or buy. A company is using the FDI build option when it incorporates a subsidiary in a foreign country, and when it hires employees and acquires offices, factories, machinery, and/or other assets in a foreign country.

> The US and Japan: American Honda Motor Co., Inc.
>
> In 1959, Honda (a Japanese corporation) established American Honda Motor Co., Inc. (AHM) as a US affiliate,[9] which was incorporated in California. The purpose of this company, which was Honda's first overseas subsidiary, was to facilitate the US distribution of motorcycles manufactured by Honda in Japan. AHM began with three employees, appointed distributors in the US, and outsourced advertising campaigns. By the early 1990s, Honda was selling twice as many cars in the US as in Japan, and AHM and its sibling and subordinate subsidiaries in the US were performing research, design, and development— and manufacturing components, motor vehicles, and other products in the US. In 2013, Honda became a net exporter of motor vehicles from the US.

---

[7] TRIMs is discussed in Chapter 8, Sections 8.4.2, 8.4.3.2, 8.5.3, and 8.5.3.2; and Chapter 9, Section 9.2.2.

[8] WTO instruments are discussed in Chapter 8, Sections 8.3 and 8.4.

[9] The term *US affiliate* is discussed in Chapter 7, Section 7.1.4.

A company is using the buy option to engage in FDI when it acquires a company, or acquires a lasting interest in a company, in a foreign country.

The US, the UK, and the UAE: Dubai Ports World

In 2005, Dubai Ports International, a United Arab Emirates (UAE) enterprise with container shipping terminal assets and operations in the Middle East, Africa, Europe, and India, paid $1.14 billion to acquire CSX World Terminals, a US corporation. This acquisition gave Dubai Ports International ownership of CSX World Terminals—and its container shipping terminal assets and operations in Australia, China, the Dominican Republic, Finland, Germany, Hong Kong, Netherlands, Puerto Rico, Russia, South Korea, the US, and Venezuela. Also in 2005, Dubai Ports International merged with Dubai Ports Authority to become Dubai Ports World (DPW). In 2006, DPW paid $6.8 billion to acquire Peninsular and Oriental Steam Navigation Company (P&O), a UK corporation and the world's fourth largest shipping terminal operator. This acquisition gave DPW ownership of P&O, its operating subsidiaries, its assets, and its 29 container shipping terminal operations in 18 countries.[10]

When either the build or buy option involves an equity joint venture (EJV) with a national of the host country, the FDI can take the form of an international strategic alliance (ISA). The use of EJV ISAs in FDI are discussed in Sections 5.3.1.2, 5.3.2, 5.4.3, and 5.5.1; and in Chapter 12, Sections 12.2.4.1 and 12.2.4.3.

5.3   FDI Industry Access Barriers

Barriers to FDI can be either industry specific or non-industry specific.[11] Most entry barriers to FDI are industry specific.

An industry-specific access barrier is any FDI barrier that restricts or prevents a foreign investor from entering an industry or industry

---

[10] DPW's acquisition of P&O is discussed in Sections 5.4.2 and 5.6.
[11] Non-industry-specific barriers to FDI are discussed in Section 5.5.2.

segment[12] in a host country.[13] Industry-specific barriers are also called *industry access barriers*. The method that is most widely used by host countries to restrict or prevent access to an industry is equity restrictions, which are also referred to as *ownership restrictions*.

5.3.1 FDI Equity Restrictions

Equity restrictions limit the percentage of the ordinary issued and outstanding shares that foreign investors are permitted to own in a company in a host country. Equity restrictions can also cover operating conditions.[14] Industries in host countries are classified as either closed or open to FDI. Open industries are classified as either unrestricted or restricted.

5.3.1.1   Closed Industries

If foreign investors are prohibited from owning equity in a company in a specific industry, this is called *full exclusion*. Fully excluded industries are also referred to as being closed to FDI.

> Industries closed to FDI
> Industries that are closed to FDI include the agriculture and forest products industries in Japan; the fishing industries in Brazil, Chile, China, Iceland, Indonesia, Italy, Japan, Saudi Arabia, and the US; the media industry in China; the real estate industries in the Czech Republic, Saudi Arabia, Slovak Republic, and Turkey; the mining industries in Iceland, Japan, and Saudi Arabia; and the electricity generation and distribution industries in Iceland and Austria.

5.3.1.2   Restricted Open Industries

The term *restricted industries* refers to open industries where the amount of foreign equity ownership is limited or is subject to conditions. The most

---

[12] Subindustry barriers to FDI are discussed in Section 5.5.1.

[13] References to *industry* can also apply to industry segments and sub-segments.

[14] Restrictions on FDI operating conditions are discussed in Section 5.3.2.

common restrictions limit FDI equity ownership to 50 percent of a company's issued and outstanding shares, or prohibit full foreign ownership of a company by requiring a minimum domestic equity ownership.

China: Car manufacturing

From 1994 until 2022, the car segment of the automotive manufacturing industry in China was restricted. During this period, governmental regulations required that, with two exceptions,[15] equity ownership by foreign investors in car manufacturing companies not exceed 50 percent. Because of this requirement, most FDI in the automotive industry in China has been through equity joint ventures. These have included the 50–50 EJV between Volkswagen and First Automotive Works, the 40–60 EJV between Volkswagen and Shanghai Automotive Industry Corporation, the 50–50 EJV between Toyota and Guangzhou Automobile Group, and the 50–50 EJV between Honda and Dongfeng Motor.

5.3.1.3   Unrestricted Open Industries

If there are no restrictions relating to the foreign ownership of equity in companies in an open industry, the industry is referred to as *unrestricted*.

Unrestricted industries

Unrestricted industries include the manufacturing, oil refining and chemicals, metals and minerals, machinery, electronic and electrical instruments, transportation equipment, electricity generation and distribution, construction, wholesale trade, and retail trade industries in the Czech Republic, Denmark, France, Germany, Hungry, Luxembourg, the Netherlands, Poland, Portugal, Romania, Slovak Republic, Spain, Sweden, and Turkey.

5.3.2   *FDI Operating Conditions*

Equity ownership restrictions can also include terms and conditions relating to a foreign investor's operations.

---

[15] The exceptions to this requirement are discussed in Sections 5.3.2 and 5.5.1.

China: Car manufacturing for export

The 50 percent equity-ownership restriction that governed FDI in the car segment of the automotive manufacturing industry in China from 1994 to 2022[16] applied to companies that marketed all or some of their products in China. If all of the vehicles produced by a car manufacturing company were for export, the foreign investor was permitted to own up to 100 percent of the company's equity. During part of the 1994 to 2022 period, Honda had two EJVs in China with Dongfeng Motor Corporation. One of these EJVs (Dongfeng Honda Automotive Company) manufactured and marketed vehicles in China. Honda's equity ownership in this EJV was 50 percent. Honda's other EJV with Dongfeng (Honda Automobile [China] Company) manufactured vehicles solely for export. Honda's equity ownership in this EJV was 65 percent.

5.4   Reasons for Restricting Access to FDI

The reasons that governments of nation-states close industries to FDI, or apply restrictions to open industries, can include: (1) to protect domestic industries and companies from foreign competition, (2) to protect national security, (3) to protect or achieve national interests, and/or (4) to protect an industry from unwanted influences.

5.4.1   Foreign Competition

The reason that drives most industry-access restrictions on FDI is the protection of domestic companies or domestic industries from foreign competition. The underlying rationale for protecting domestic companies and industries from FDI are the same as, or similar to, the rationale for the protectionist use of tariffs, NTBs, and other barriers to trade.[17]

---

[16] This restriction is discussed in the example in Section 5.3.1.2.

[17] The protectionist uses of tariffs, NTBs, and other barriers to trade are discussed in Chapter 2, Section 2.4.1; Chapter 3, Section 3.2.4; and Chapter 4, Section 4.3.1.

5.4.2 *National Security*

The governments of most nation-states have policies and procedures that restrict FDI that could potentially threaten national security, even if the FDI would be in an open industry.

The US: The CFIUS

The responsibility for deciding if a foreign direct investor poses a threat to US national security rests with the Committee on Foreign Investment in the United States (CFIUS).[18] The members of this committee represent 12 government departments and agencies: the Treasury; the Departments of State, Defense, Commerce, Homeland Security, and Justice; the Office of Management and Budget; the Council of Economic Advisors; the National Security Council; the National Economic Council; the Office of Science and Technology Policy; and the US Trade Representative.[19] The CFIUS is chaired by the Secretary of the Treasury.

The US: DPW and P&O

In 2005, prior to DPW's acquisition of P&O,[20] DPW and P&O contacted the CFIUS because P&O operated shipping terminals in Baltimore, Miami, New Jersey, New Orleans, New York, and Philadelphia, and in 16 other US ports—and because DPW and P&O believed the "proposed transaction could raise national security issues that should appropriately be reviewed by the US Government."[21] This initiative was followed by DPW and P&O briefings for CFIUS members, independent analyses by each of the CFIUS member departments and agencies, a request for an intelligence assessment of DPW by the CFIUS, and the negotiation of an assurances letter with the companies by the Department of Homeland Security.

---

[18] The CFIUS was created by Section 721 of the Defense Production Act of 1950, which is referred to as the *Exon-Florio amendment*.

[19] In some cases, the Departments of Energy and Transportation, the Nuclear Regulatory Agency, and other US agencies participate in CFIUS reviews.

[20] DPW's acquisition of P&O is discussed in Sections 5.2.2 and 5.6.

[21] USDOT, Dubai-P&OE-F Fact Sheet.

5.4.3   National Interest

In some cases, the reason a national government gives for restricting industry access is the national interest. This is an extremely broad term that can include criteria related to economic development, creating or preserving employment, and/or effecting technology transfer.

China: Car manufacturing and technology transfer

Because equity joint ventures and other forms of strategic alliances are a highly practical and proven mechanism for effecting technology transfer, the government of China has adopted a policy of encouraging and in some cases mandating the use of international strategic alliances to achieve China's economic development goals. One of the reasons for the 50 percent equity-ownership restriction on FDI in car manufacturing companies in China, from 1994 to 2022, was to facilitate the transfer of manufacturing and managerial technology from foreign-funded companies[22] to Chinese-funded companies.

5.4.4   Unwanted Influences

In some cases, governments of nation-states prohibit or restrict industry-specific FDI—for the purpose of protecting an industry or their society from unwanted foreign cultural, social, or political influence.

The media industries in China and France

In China, the media industry is closed to FDI; in France, FDI in the media industry is severely restricted. The reasons appear to be related to these countries wanting to limit foreign cultural, social, or political influence in their media industries.

5.4.5   Combinations and Disguised Restrictions

In some cases, the decision by a national government to restrict or prohibit FDI in an industry may be motivated by a combination of two

---

[22] The term *foreign-funded company* is discussed in Chapter 7, Section 7.1.4.

or more reasons. For example, in some countries, specific industries are reserved for commercial enterprises that are owned or controlled by the national government—which are referred to as *state-owned enterprises* (SOEs).[23] This reservation may be due to a combination of national security and national interest reasons, but may also be for (or influenced by) social, cultural, political, or economic reasons.

It can be difficult to determine the principal reason for some industry-specific barriers because in many cases a host-country government does not give a reason for imposing a restriction, or, as in the case of NTBs, because it may be a disguised restriction.[24]

5.4.6   *No or Low Industry Restrictions*

Data developed by the OECD show that the most open industries (i.e., the industries with no FDI equity-ownership restrictions or the lowest FDI equity-ownership restrictions) are manufacturing industries. The reason many developing countries[25] impose no or low barriers on foreign access to these industries is because FDI in manufacturing can:

- Generate investment capital;
- Create employment;
- Provide employees with vocational knowledge and skills;
- Facilitate the transfer of managerial and manufacturing technology;
- Result in import substitution (which benefits a host country's balance of trade and balance of payments by reducing the need for imports); and
- Result in an increase in exports (which benefits a host country's balance of trade and balance of payments).

---

[23] In practice, the term *state-owned enterprise* (SOE) is also used when referring to an enterprise that is owned or controlled by the government of a territorial sub-unit within a nation-state—such as a state, provincial, county, or municipal government.

[24] The term *disguised restriction* is from Article XX of the GATT, and is discussed in Chapter 3, Section 3.2.4.

[25] Developing countries are discussed in Chapter 7, Section 7.1.2.2.

The exception to the relative openness of manufacturing industries is those industries that are closed because of national security, or closed or restricted because of national interests.

5.5   Industry Specificity and FDI

Most entry barriers to FDI are industry specific. Entry barriers to FDI can, however, also be subindustry specific and non-industry specific.

5.5.1   Subindustry-Specific Entry Barriers

In some cases, different segments within the same industry have different levels of industry access or have different equity ownership restrictions.

China: Car and car-engine manufacturing

Toyota (a Japanese corporation) has equity joint ventures with several companies in China that manufacture and market cars, trucks, and buses—including Guangzhou Automobile Group. The equity ownership in each of these EJVs is 50–50. Toyota also has a separate EJV with Guangzhou Automobile Group that manufactures engines, which are used in the manufacture of its cars in China, North America, Europe, and Japan. Toyota's equity ownership in this EJV is 70 percent. This is permitted, because the 50 percent auto-industry equity ownership limit in China[26] does not apply to the engine manufacturing segment of the automotive industry.

5.5.2   Non-Industry-Specific Entry Barriers

Non-industry-specific barriers to FDI are barriers that apply to FDI in any and all industries, and to any and all segments or sub-segments within an industry. For example, some countries have minimum

---

[26] This equity ownership limit is discussed in Sections 5.3.1.2 and 5.3.2.

investment requirements, which apply more or less equally to all industries.

Kenya: FDI approval

The government of Kenya says there are no entry barriers for FDI in Kenya. But the approval requirements contained in Kenya's Investment Promotion Act states that, to receive approval from the Kenya Investment Authority, an FDI application must be for not less than US$500,000.

If a foreign company intends to engage in large-scale manufacturing, minimum investment requirements do not act as an entry barrier to FDI. But if a foreign company intends to establish small manufacturing operations; to engage in warehousing, assembly and/or distribution operations that are associated with international trade; or to enter a service industry or some other non-capital-intensive industry—then minimum investment requirements can act as an entry barrier to FDI.

Non-industry-specific barriers to FDI also include currency and financial restrictions and requirements, human resources restrictions and requirements, and landownership restrictions.[27] Because these FDI barriers restrict or regulate the operations of FDI after it has entered the commerce of a host country, they are classified as "post-entry barriers to FDI," which are discussed in Chapter 6.

5.6   The Politicization of Entry Barriers to FDI

The politicization of a government's regulatory authority can result in barriers to trade and FDI. The politicization of trade barriers is discussed in Chapter 4, Section 4.4. The politicization of post-entry barriers to FDI is discussed in Chapter 6, Section 6.5. The politicization of entry barriers to FDI is discussed in this section.

---

[27] Currency and financial restrictions and requirements are discussed in Chapter 6, Section 6.2.1. Human resources restrictions and requirements are discussed in Chapter 6, Sections 6.2.3 and 6.3.1.3.

5.6.1   *The Politicization of FDI Entry Approvals*

The politicization of a government's regulatory authority can include the politicized treatment of a foreign-funded company that is applying for approval to acquire an entity in a host country—or to acquire an entity that has operations in a host country.

The US: DPW and P&O

In the acquisition of P&O by DPW (which is discussed in Sections 5.2.2 and 5.4.2 of this chapter), P&O was not a US entity—but DPW and P&O applied to the CFIUS for approval, because P&O had extensive operations in the US. At the end of the process discussed in Section 5.4.2, "all CFIUS members agreed that this particular transaction should be allowed to proceed,"[28] and the application by DPW and P&O was approved unanimously by the CFIUS. On March 7, 2006, almost two months after the CFIUS completed its review of the transaction and approved the transaction, DPW completed its acquisition of P&O.

But the acquisition was opposed by some members of the US Congress. On March 8, 2006, the House Appropriations Committee voted 62 to 2 to block DPW from acquiring P&O's port operations in the US. On March 9, DPW announced it would divest all of P&O's US port operations. In December 2006, DPW completed the divestiture of its US port operations to AIG Global Investment Group, the investment subsidiary of American International Group (a US corporation).

Because the CFIUS is an inter-departmental agency of the US government, which is chaired by the Secretary of the Treasury and includes representation from 12 offices, agencies, and departments of the US government[29]—and because DPW's application to acquire P&O was approved unanimously by the CFIUS, this approval would indicate that DPW's application satisfied all of the government's regulatory

---

[28] USDOT, Dubai-P&OE-F Fact Sheet.
[29] The members of the CFIUS are listed in Section 5.4.2.

requirements. The action by the House Appropriations Committee to override the CFIUS approval and to block DPW's acquisition of P&Os port operations in the United States was a political action—and was, therefore, an example of the politicization of an entry barrier to FDI.

5.6.2   Types of FDI Political Risk Exposures

FDI political risk[30] exposures, which include the politicization of entry barriers to FDI, and the politicized treatment of foreign-funded companies, can be: (1) industry specific, (2) home-country specific, and/or (3) company specific.[31] The politicization of an FDI entry barrier can also be a combination of two or, in some cases, all three of these specificities.

The US: DPW and P&O

The arguments in the US media by members of the US Congress indicate that the politicization of DPW's acquisition of P&O by the House Appropriations Committee was both industry specific (the US shipping terminals industry) and home-country specific (the UAE). Some of the media statements by Members of Congress argued that, because DPW is a state-owned enterprise,[32] their failure to block DPW would mean that a foreign government would be operating US ports, which would indicate that the politicization was also company specific.

5.6.3   Severity and Frequency

The severity of the adverse affects of political risk exposures that result from the politicization of entry barriers to FDI, is (as with trade-related political risks[33]) relatively low. In the DPW case, the US governmental action that prevented DPW from operating shipping terminals at six

---

[30] The term *political risk* is defined and discussed in Chapter 4, Section 4.4.1.
[31] These three types of political risk exposures are discussed in Chapter 6, Section 6.5.5.
[32] State-owned enterprises (SOEs) are discussed in Section 5.4.5.
[33] The severity of trade-related political risks is discussed in Chapter 4, Section 4.4.2.

major ports and 16 other ports in the US was a lost opportunity cost for DPW. But the US governmental action did not prevent DPW from acquiring P&O, and DPW's divestiture of US port operations to AIG Global Investment Group meant that DPW was not encumbered with an unusable asset. Also, the governmental actions in the DPW case increased the difficulty and costs associated with the conduct of DPW's FDI in the US—but these governmental actions did not (as with trade-related political risks) result in the loss of control or ownership of an entity's assets or investment.[34]

The frequency of the politicization of entry barriers to FDI is difficult to determine. The disclosure of information concerning the DPW case notwithstanding, governments generally do not make public information related to rejected FDI applications, whether or not the reasons for rejection are politicized. And enterprises do not usually publicize their failures, which includes not publicizing their failures to receive FDI approvals. It is, therefore, difficult or impossible to know how many FDI applications are rejected because of politicization, or how many FDI applications are not made by potential foreign direct investors to avoid the possibility of a politicized rejection.

---

[34] Political risk-related loss of control or ownership is discussed in Chapter 6, Sections 6.5.2.2, 6.5.3, and 6.5.4.

CHAPTER 6

Post-Entry Barriers to FDI

Contents

6.1   Introduction

The term *post-entry barriers to FDI* refers to barriers that restrict or regulate the conduct of FDI after it has entered the commerce of a host country. The sources and types of post-entry barriers to FDI include legislated barriers, contract-specific barriers, administrative barriers, and political risk barriers.

Some post-entry barriers to FDI can act as non-tariff barriers to trade, and are the same as or similar to some of the NTBs discussed in Chapter 3, Section 3.3. Some entry barriers to FDI (such as equity ownership restrictions and operating conditions related to equity ownership[1]) can act as post-entry barriers to FDI. And some post-entry barriers to FDI can also act as entry barriers to FDI—because they influence a company's decision to invest, or not to invest, in a host country.[2]

---

[1] These equity restrictions to FDI are discussed in Chapter 5, Section 5.3.1.
[2] This is discussed in Section 6.4.4.

6.2   Legislated Barriers to FDI

Laws that govern FDI operations in a host country, which are created by the legislative branch of the host-country government, can act as post-entry barriers to FDI. Legislated barriers to FDI apply to all foreign-funded companies operating in a host country,[3] unless a law specifically addresses FDI in a specific industry or a specific segment of an industry. Legislated barriers include: (1) currency and financial restrictions, (2) local-content requirements, (3) human resources restrictions and requirements, and (4) landownership restrictions.

6.2.1   *Currency and Financial Barriers*

Currency differences and financial issues can complicate the conduct of FDI. But, in some cases, currency and financial issues function as barriers to FDI, which can include: (1) restrictions on the convertibility of currencies, (2) restrictions on the repatriation of profits and capital, and (3) other financial operating barriers.

6.2.1.1   The Convertibility of Currencies

The governments of many countries, and especially the governments of developing countries,[4] attempt to limit the outflow of capital by limiting the convertibility of their currencies.

6.2.1.2   The Repatriation of Profits and Capital

The term *repatriation of funds* refers to the transfer of funds from a host country to a foreign investor's home country.[5] Some countries,

---

[3] As discussed in Chapter 7, Section 7.1.4, if the nationality of an entity's principal shareholder(s) is different from the entity's country of incorporation, the entity can be called a *foreign-funded company*.

[4] Developing countries are discussed in Chapter 7, Section 7.1.2.2.

[5] The terms *host country* and *home country* are discussed in Chapter 7, Section 7.1.2.1.

and especially developing countries, have laws and/or regulations that prohibit or limit the repatriation of profits and/or capital. Although the term *repatriation* refers specifically to the transfer of funds to a foreign-funded company's home country (its *patria*), in practice repatriation restrictions prevent funds from leaving the host country and being remitted to any other country. In some cases, restrictions on the repatriation of profits and capital delay, rather than prevent, the international movement of funds.

6.2.1.3   Other Financial Operating Barriers

A company's FDI operations can also be adversely affected by other financial operating barriers. These can include administrative and processing fees or taxes, annual license renewal fees, and taxes on foreign remittances.[6]

6.2.1.4   Payments for Imports

NTBs include restrictions on payments for imports.[7] Because these restrictions can make it difficult for an FDI manufacturing entity in a host country to import necessary materials and components, the currency and financial restrictions and requirements can, in some cases, also act as post-entry barriers to FDI.

6.2.2   Local-Content Requirements

To maximize the benefits that FDI in manufacturing can contribute to the economic development of a host country,[8] some host-country governments have adopted laws and/or regulations that require foreign-funded manufacturers to use not less than a certain level of domestically produced materials and components, and/or to progressively increase the

---

[6] Administrative barriers are discussed in Section 6.4.

[7] See Chapter 3, Section 3.3.1, Item 1.

[8] These benefits are discussed in Chapter 5, Section 5.4.6.

level of local content used in their manufacturing operations. Local-content requirements can include: (1) legislated local-content requirements, which can be industry specific or subindustry specific; and (2) company-specific and contract-specific local-content requirements.[9] The use of local-content requirements by WTO members is restricted by Article XI, General Elimination of Quantitative Restrictions, of the GATT, and by the provisions contained in the "Agreement on Trade-Related Investment Measures."[10]

6.2.3 Human Resources Regulations

The term *human resources indigenization* refers to the requirement by a host country government that foreign direct investors appoint nationals of the host country to specific managerial positions, and/or refers to the mandatory phased replacement of senior-level employees who are foreign nationals with employees who are host-country nationals.[11] Human resources (HR) barriers that affect FDI operations can be classified as: (1) legislated HR requirements, or (2) company-specific HR requirements.[12] Legislated HR requirements are contained in laws that place general restrictions on the employment of foreign nationals[13] and apply to all foreign-funded companies in a host country.

Malaysia: Ethnic employee requirement

Before 2009, Malaysia's New Economic Policy required that foreign-funded companies "allocate 30 percent of their staff positions to ethnic Malays," who make up about 60 percent of

---

[9] Contract-specific local-content requirements are discussed in Section 6.3.1.1.

[10] TRIMs is discussed in Chapter 8, Sections 8.4.2, 8.4.3.2, 8.5.3, and 8.5.3.2; and Chapter 9, Section 9.2.2.

[11] The terms *foreign national* and *host-country national* are discussed in Chapter 7, Section 7.1.2.1.

[12] Company-specific HR requirements are discussed in Section 6.3.1.3.

[13] An individual who is not a host-country national can be called a *foreign national*, or as a *non-national*. These terms are discussed in Chapter 7, Section 7.1.2.1.

the country's population. This requirement was discontinued in 2009, following the implementation of "a new investor-friendly economic model."[14]

Legislated HR requirements can limit the number or percentage of foreign nationals a company is permitted to employ, and/or can limit the number or percentage of foreign nationals who hold positions in specific categories. The employment of persons who are foreign nationals can be made more complex and difficult because of a host country's application and approval requirements and processes.[15] In some cases, legislated HR requirements apply to both domestic and foreign-funded companies—but can be more problematic for foreign-funded companies and their parent companies that often need to move managers, executives, legal counsel, and technical personnel between countries where they have operations. The use of human resources indigenization requirements has declined since the adoption of the 1994 "Agreement on Trade-Related Investment Measures."[16] Also, some preferential trade agreements (PTAs)[17] prohibit the use of these requirements.

The RCEP Agreement

Article 10.7: Senior Management and Board of Directors, of the "Regional Comprehensive Economic Partnership (RCEP) Agreement,"[18] states in Paragraph (1) that RCEP members not require a foreign direct investor to appoint "to a senior management position a natural person of any particular nationality." Paragraph (2) states that members not require that a majority of an FDI board of directors, or a committee of an FDI board of directors, be of a particular nationality.

---

[14] Associated Press. n.d. "Malaysia Relaxes Investment Rules."
[15] Application and approval requirements and processes are discussed in Section 6.4.1.
[16] TRIMs is discussed in Chapter 8, Sections 8.4.2, 8.4.3.2, 8.5.3, and 8.5.3.2; and Chapter 9, Section 9.2.2.
[17] PTAs are discussed in Chapter 7, Section 7.1.6.
[18] The RCEP Agreement is discussed in Chapter 7, Section 7.3.2.1.

6.2.4 Landownership and Leasing Restrictions

Some countries have laws and/or regulations that prevent or restrict the ownership of land by foreign-funded companies. In developing countries, many of these laws and regulations date from the Mexican Constitution of 1917 and Mexico's land reform program, the adoption of Resolution GS 1803 on the Permanent Sovereignty over Natural Resources by the General Assembly of the United Nations in 1962, and the rise in post-colonial nationalism that began in the early 1960s.[19] These landownership barriers are in most cases not industry specific, but can be especially problematic for FDI in some industries.

For foreign-funded companies engaged in agriculture or manufacturing, landownership restrictions can prevent them from buying farms or factories, and can severely limit their ability to acquire land on which to develop farms or to build factories. Some countries that restrict land ownership by foreign-funded companies allow real estate to be leased. But leasing may not be operationally feasible, because a foreign-funded company may be reluctant to invest in improvements to real estate it does not own. The operational feasibility of leasing can be further exacerbated by concerns that, if there is a dispute with a property owner, the property owner may receive preferential treatment by the hostcountry government and/or by the host country's courts.[20] In some cases, a host country's laws and/or regulations prohibit foreign-funded companies from leasing land for agricultural use.

> Kenya: Land ownership and leasing restrictions
>
> The Kenya Land Control Act prohibits non-citizen enterprises, and joint ventures that include non-citizens, from owning or leasing agricultural land. The Kenya Land Control Act provides, however, that the president of Kenya can grant exemptions to these restrictions.[21]

---

[19] These factors are discussed in Section 6.5.2.1.

[20] The possibility of host-country nationals receiving preferential treatment in international commercial disputes is discussed in Chapter 12, Section 12.2.1.2.

[21] This exemption is discussed in Section 6.4.3.

6.3   Contract-Specific Barriers to FDI

An FDI agreement is a contract between a foreign direct investor and the government of a host country. The terms and conditions of FDI agreements can result in post-entry barriers to FDI. These terms and conditions apply only to the FDI that is covered by the agreement, and apply only to the foreign-funded company that is a party to the agreement.

6.3.1   Performance Requirements

Agreements between foreign direct investors and the governments of host countries include an almost infinite range of terms and conditions. There is, however, a small group of terms and conditions, called *performance requirements*, that frequently act as post-entry barriers to FDI. The term *performance requirement* refers to a quantitative level of performance in a specified functional area that must be achieved by an FDI's operations within a specific time period. Performance requirements can include: (1) local-content requirements, (2) export-quota requirements, (3) human resources indigenization requirements, and (4) environmental impact requirements. The restrictions on the use of local-content and export-quota requirements by WTO members, which are discussed in Section 6.2.2, also apply to contract-specific, local-content, and export-quota requirements.

6.3.1.1   Local Content

Some host-country governments have adopted laws and/or regulations that require foreignfunded manufacturers to use a certain level of domestically produced materials and components.[22] Some host-country governments, however, make local-content requirements contract specific—by including local-content schedules in FDI agreements—or by using a combination of legislated and contract-specific local-content requirements. Local-content schedules require foreign-funded companies, over time, to progressively increase the level of local content used in their

---

[22] See Section 6.2.2.

manufacturing operations. These schedules usually specify what percentage of the total-content value, and what percentage of each category of materials or parts, must be local content by each time milestone specified in the agreement.

6.3.1.2   Export Quotas

Because FDI in manufacturing can generate exports, and because exports benefit a host country's balance of trade and balance of payments,[23] some host-country governments attempt to maximize the exports by foreign-funded manufacturers by including minimum export quotas in their FDI agreements.[24] Export quota requirements are usually contained in a schedule that specifies the percentage of the foreign investor's output, in each category, that must be exported during each time period covered in the agreement.

6.3.1.3   Human Resources Indigenization

Human resources indigenization restrictions and requirements can be classified as: (1) legislated HR requirements, or (2) company-specific HR requirements.[25] In host countries that have company-specific indigenization requirements, these requirements are usually contained in an indigenization schedule, which is part of a foreign-funded company's FDI agreement. An indigenization schedule specifies the minimum number or percentage of managers, executives, and technical experts in each category, at each level, who must be host-country nationals (or the maximum number or percentage of allowable foreign nationals) by specified time milestones.

Compliance with indigenization requirements has been problematic for some foreign direct investors, and especially for progressive well-managed foreign-funded companies that have provided for their managers, executives, and technical experts who are host-country

---

[23] These benefits are discussed in Chapter 5, Section 5.4.6.

[24] Quotas are discussed in Chapter 3, Section 3.3.2.

[25] This is discussed in Section 6.2.3.

nationals to receive advanced levels of professional education, training, and certification. The improved credentials that have resulted from these company-sponsored employee development practices have, in some cases, contributed to the loss of host-country national employees to other companies or even to the host-country government, which has resulted in the foreign direct investor that has lost the employee(s) being out of compliance with the indigenization terms of their FDI contract.

The use of contract-specific human resources indigenization requirements, as with their legislated equivalent, has declined since the adoption of TRIMs and some regional PTAs.

6.3.1.4   Environmental Impact

The increase in the emphasis on environmental protection has resulted in the governments of some hostcountries including environmental-impact performance requirements in their FDI agreements.

6.3.2   Penalties

The penalties for noncompliance with performance requirements are stated in a host-country's FDI laws and/or regulations, and/or in the provisions contained in company-specific FDI agreements. The most serious penalties can include the revocation of a company's FDI approvals by a host-country government, which results in the termination of the company's operations in the host country and the partial or total loss of its investment.

6.4   Administrative Barriers to FDI

The implementation of the laws and/or regulations that govern FDI operations in a host country requires the use of administrative regulations, which are created and administered by the executive branch of the host-country government. In some cases, administrative regulations, and related decisions and actions, can act as post-entry barriers to FDI. Administrative barriers include: (1) application and approval requirements and processes, (2) the lack of transparency, and (3) the absence of established procedures.

6.4.1 Applications and Approvals

Some of the least recognized but most problematic post-entry barriers to trade and FDI are governmental application and approval requirements, and related processes. These requirements and processes can increase the cost, complexity, and difficulty of operating in a host country.

6.4.2 Transparency

When referring to political and governmental structures, systems, and processes, the term *transparency* refers to openness and the availability of information related to: (1) the criteria used when making decisions and (2) the identity and roles of the government departments and personnel who participate in decision-making processes.

> The EU: Decision-related transparency
>
> On its "transparency portal" web page, the EU says decisions affecting European citizens' lives "must be taken as openly as possible. As a European citizen, you have a right to know how the European institutions are preparing these decisions, who participates in preparing them, who receives funding from the EU budget, and what documents are held or produced to prepare and adopt the legal acts. You also have a right to access those documents."[26]

The first function of transparency processes is to facilitate public access to information. Other functions of transparency processes include measures to avoid conflicts of interests by persons who participate in or oversee decision-making—and measures to ensure that these persons do not act in self-interest. The lack of transparency is often associated with corruption in government, which can be defined as the abuse of governmental authority or power for gain by an individual or group.

6.4.3 Established Procedures

In some host countries, there is a tendency for governmental decision-making to be autocratic or arbitrary, and to be characterized by an absence of established procedures.

---

[26] European Commission, EU Transparency Portal.

Kenya: Exemptions

The Kenya Land Control Act allows the president of Kenya to grant exemptions to restrictions that prohibit non-citizen enterprises, and joint ventures that include non-citizens, from owning or leasing agricultural land.[27] But this act and other governmental documents say nothing about the process for applying for an exemption. These documents also say nothing about the criteria that the government and the president will use when assessing exemption applications, and contain no information about the positions or identities of the persons in the government who evaluate exemption applications and advise the president concerning the approval of exemptions.

As with the lack of transparency, the absence of established procedures is often associated with corruption in government.

6.4.4   Barriers to Trade and FDI

The lack of transparency and the absence of established procedures can act as entry and post-entry barriers to both trade and FDI, because they make it difficult or impossible for managers, executives, legal counsel, and board members at foreign-funded companies to know:

- How governmental decisions are made;
- What criteria are used in making governmental decisions;
- What government departments and personnel participate in the decision-making processes; and
- What is the specific decision-making role and authority of participating departments and personnel.

The lack of transparency and the absence of established procedures are reflected in some of the NTBs associated with administrative regulations, which are discussed in Chapter 3, Section 3.3.1.

---

[27] This is discussed in Section 6.2.4.

6.5   The Politicization of Post-entry Barriers to FDI

The politicization of a government's regulatory authority can result in barriers to both trade and FDI. The politicization of trade barriers is discussed in Chapter 4, Section 4.4. The politicization of entry barriers to FDI is discussed in Chapter 5, Section 5.6. The politicization of post-entry barriers to FDI is discussed in this section.

6.5.1   Political Risk

When an entity that is engaged in the practice of international trade and/or FDI is exposed to the adverse effects that could result from the politicization of a government's regulatory authority, this exposure is called *political risk*.[28]

Political risk can include an exposure to an action by a government's legislative, executive, or judicial branch (and to combinations of actions by these branches of a government); to an exposure to the politicized treatment of an enterprise, its shareholders, its assets, and/or its trade and/or FDI operations; and to the politicized prejudicial application of post-entry barriers to FDI—which can adversely affect the survival, success, and sustainability of a foreign-funded company, its operations, and/or its parent company.[29]

Exposures to post-entry FDI political risk can include the expropriation, nationalization,[30] or unilateral renegotiation[31] of a foreign-funded company, its assets, and/or its FDI operations—and the politicization of post-entry administrative barriers to FDI, which can add to the difficulty and/or cost of doing business by a foreign-funded company.

---

[28] This is discussed in Chapter 4, Section 4.4.1.

[29] Davies. n.d. "Beyond the Earthquake Allegory: Managing Political Risk Vulnerability."

[30] Expropriation and nationalization are discussed in Sections 6.5.3.1, 6.5.3.2, and 6.5.4.1.

[31] Unilateral renegotiation is discussed in Sections 6.5.3.3 and 6.5.4.2.

6.5.2 Historical Antecedents

In international business, the term *political risk* was originally used when referring to the possibility of the expropriation or nationalization of an FDI operation in a developing country by the host-country government.[32] The conditions that led to these politicized actions began following the decolonization of more than 50 non-self-governing territories[33] between 1950 and 1965; to the manifestation of post-colonial nationalism in these newly independent developing countries; and to similar actions by the governments of other developing countries.

Beginning in the early 1960s and continuing through the end of the 1970s, post-colonial nationalism and political activism within many newly independent countries led to a large number of political coups for which the period became famous. During this period, many leaders of newly independent countries blamed the government of their former metropole[34] for having entered into agreements with foreign direct investors (and especially foreign direct investors who were nationals of the former metropole) that allowed these investors to operate under terms that were unfavorable to the host country, and in some cases were blatantly exploitative.

Also, during this period, the governments of many newly independent countries repudiated the principle of sanctity of contract; refused to respect unfavorable conditions contained in FDI agreements; and either changed those unfavorable parts of agreements by unilaterally renegotiating them, or, in some cases, by expropriating or nationalizing the FDI's operations, its assets, and/or the entity. These repudiation behaviors by the governments of recently decolonized countries were accompanied by similar behaviors by the governments of other developing countries that

---

[32] The term *host country government* is discussed in Chapter 7, Section 7.1.2.1.

[33] The term *non-self-governing territories* (NSGTs) is contained in Chapter XI of the UN Charter. Article 73 of the charter requires that UN member states provide information on NSGTs for which they "have or assume responsibilities." The first list of NSGTs was compiled by the UN General Assembly in 1946, and included 72 NSGTs.

[34] In current usage, the term *metropole* refers to a colony's home or parent country.

had been independent for decades—or, in some cases, for more than a century.

Venezuela: Oil, iron, and steel

Venezuela declared independence from Spain in 1811. In 1960, the government of Venezuela unilaterally renegotiated its FDI agreements with foreign-funded oil companies, which dramatically increased the government's share of those companies' operating profits. One of the conditions of these renegotiations was that any company that did not agree to the new terms would be expropriated, which led to the expropriation of one US-funded company. In 1975, Venezuela nationalized its iron and steel industry, and in 1976 nationalized its oil industry.

During the repudiation phase of post-colonial nationalism, developing countries (that, in 1967, became the United Nations Group of 77) were refuting the right of developed countries to act as the sole authors and arbiters of legitimate jurisprudence.

6.5.2.1   The Legal Arguments

During the repudiation phase of post-colonial nationalism, developing countries used three juridical principles to support their treatment of foreign direct investment. These were: (1) that agreements are subject to things being the same; (2) that disputes must be settled by the courts of the country in which they occur; and (3) that natural resources are the permanent property of the state.

- *Rebus sic stantibus*

  The dictum that agreements are subject to things being the same, *rebus sic stantibus*, was invoked as the essential antithesis to the sanctity of contract principle, *pacta sunt servunda*.
  Given that change was the pervading ethos of the repudiation phase of post-colonial nationalism, it was relatively easy for host-country governments to justify their FDI-related actions by invoking *rebus sic stantibus*. For example, the long time

frames for oil operations, and exceptionally long time frames
for mining operations, made oil and mining agreements
especially vulnerable to negation or unilateral renegotiation,
on the grounds that things had changed.

- *Locus regit actum*
  The argument that disputes must be decided by the national
  courts of the country in which they occur was based on the
  jurisdictional principle *locus regit actum*, and the principle of
  the exhaustion of local remedies. These principles hold that
  disputes must be decided by local courts, and that all local
  procedures, including appeals, must be exhausted before
  a dispute is taken to an extra-national dispute settlement
  mechanism.[35] This emphasis on the primacy of national courts
  had been argued in the mid-19th century by Argentinian
  jurist Carlos Calvo (who went further and denied the
  jurisdiction of extra-national courts under any circumstances).
  During the repudiation phase of post-colonial nationalism,
  this principle came to be called the *Calvo Doctrine*, and was
  used to negate the dispute settlement clauses of FDI contracts
  that provided for disputes to be settled by the courts of a
  company's home country, by third-country courts, or by
  supra-national arbitration.

- The permanent sovereignty of natural resources
  The principle of the permanent sovereignty[36] of natural
  resources first appeared in Article 27 of the Mexican
  Constitution of 1917, as the constitutional basis for
  that government's land reform program, and appeared
  subsequently in the constitution of Venezuela and in the
  constitutions of other developing countries. In 1958, the
  United Nations established a Commission on the Permanent
  Sovereignty of Natural Resources and, in 1962, the UN
  General Assembly adopted a resolution on the Permanent

---

[35] The exhaustion of local remedies is discussed in Chapter 12, Section 12.4.3.
[36] Sovereignty is discussed in Chapter 7, Section 7.1.5.

Sovereignty of Natural Resources (GA 1803). In 1974, the UN adopted the "Declaration on the Establishment of the New Economic Order" (GA 3201) and the "Charter of Economic Rights and Duties of States" (GA 3281).[37] These resolutions provided for "the right of peoples and nations to permanent sovereignty over their natural wealth and resources" and "the right of all states freely to dispose of their natural wealth and resources in accordance with their national interests." Operationally, GA 1803, GA 3201, and GA 3281 were used to cover the confiscations of oil and mining FDI properties for the next 15 years.

6.5.2.2   From Confiscation to Control

By the beginning of the 1980s, most senior-level political leaders in developing countries that were host-countries to FDI had come to believe in the priority of economic development, and to believe that their countries could not achieve economic development without FDI from developed countries. Also, they were learning that it was difficult or impossible to attract foreign capital and foreign-funded entities if they continued to repudiate the principle of sanctity of contract, to espouse the legal arguments outlined in the previous section—and especially if they continued to confiscate (through expropriation or nationalization) the operations and/or assets of foreign direct investors.

A combination of these factors resulted in a diminution in the repudiation of traditional norms by the leaders of the governments of developing countries—and the beginning of the reconciliation phase of post-colonial nationalism. The reconciliation phase was characterized by a vast scaling back of confiscatory behavior by the governments of developing countries, and by a shift to the use of legislative and regulatory controls.

---

[37] "Charter of Economic Rights and Duties of States" (GA 3281). December 12, 1974.

6.5.3   *Forms of Post-entry Exposures*

Post-entry FDI exposures to political risk can be grouped into four forms: expropriation, nationalization, unilateral renegotiation, and the politicization of administrative barriers.

6.5.3.1   Expropriation

In the field of international commerce, the terms *expropriation* and *nationalization* both refer to the confiscation of a foreign-funded company, its assets, and/or its FDI operations by a host-country government. The term *expropriation* refers to a situation where the owners of a confiscated company do not receive compensation.

> Venezuela: Owens Illinois
>   In 2010, the government of Venezuela expropriated the in-country glass-making operations of Owens Illinois, a Fortune 500 company and a US national, and paid the parent company no compensation.

6.5.3.2   Nationalization

The term *nationalization* is used when referring to a situation where the owners of a confiscated company receive compensation.

> Venezuela: AES
>   In 2007, the government of Venezuela nationalized the in-country assets of AES Corporation (a US national) and acquired the company's 82 percent equity interest in Electricidad de Caracas, Venezuela's largest privately owned electrical power company. Following the nationalization, the government of Venezuela paid AES $740 million in compensation.

6.5.3.3   Unilateral Renegotiation

The term *unilateral renegotiation* is a euphemism and an oxymoron. The unilateral renegotiation of an FDI agreement (which is sometimes called *partial-confiscation, quasi-confiscation,* or *creeping confiscation*) occurs when a host-country government changes the terms and conditions of an FDI agreement without first consulting the foreign direct investor, and without the consent of the foreign direct investor—and in direct contravention of the provisions for amendment contained in the agreement.

Indonesia

Before 1980, the FDI agreements between the government of Indonesia and six foreign-funded oil companies provided that the royalties to be paid to Indonesia were to be 5 percent. In 1980, the government of Indonesia unilaterally changed all of these FDI agreements, so that the royalties would be 90 percent. The Indonesian government justified this change based on their estimates of the oil companies' current costs of production—which calculations did not include the investors' exploration costs, nor their start-up costs related to the establishment of extractive, transportation, and storage infrastructures.

6.5.3.4 The Politicization of Administrative Barriers

The politicization of governmental administrative barriers to FDI include: (1) the politicization of one or more of the elements of an entry approval process;[38] and (2) the politicization of one or more of the administrative post-entry barriers to FDI that are discussed in Section 6.4 of this chapter—and especially the politicization of post-entry application and approval requirements and processes. Also, the absence of established procedures is often associated with corruption in government and the politicization of post-entry barriers to FDI.[39]

6.5.4 *Severity and Frequency*

The forms of post-entry exposures to political risk that are discussed in Section 6.5.3 are arranged in their order of severity—which approximates their reversed order of frequency.

---

[38] The politicization of these processes is discussed in Chapter 5, Section 5.6.1.
[39] This is discussed in Section 6.4.3.

6.5.4.1   Expropriation and Nationalization

The most severe forms of post-entry FDI political risk exposures are expropriation and nationalization, because both of these forms result in the loss of FDI operations and/or the FDI investment. Nationalization is seen as being less severe than expropriation, because it includes compensation (even though the compensation may be delayed, and may not be considered to be fair or adequate).

The frequency of these two forms of political risk is low. Determining the frequency of these forms is not difficult, because (unlike the general obscurity of the politicization of entry barriers to FDI[40]) entities engaged in the conduct of FDI are not able to avoid making public expropriation and nationalism actions by host governments. The reasons for the reduced frequency of these forms of political risk are an extension of the factors discussed in Section 6.5.2.2. Also, some international instruments now address, either directly or indirectly, expropriation and nationalization.

The RCEP Agreement

Article 10.13: Expropriation, Paragraph (1), of the RCEP Agreement[41] says that "No party shall expropriate or nationalize a covered investment either directly or through measures equivalent to expropriation or nationalization except: (a) for a public purpose; (b) in a non-discriminatory manner; (c) on payment of compensation ...; and (d) in accordance with due process of law." The paragraphs that follow say that compensation "shall be paid without delay" and "be equivalent to the fair market value of the expropriated investment."

Annex 10B: Expropriation, of the RCEP Agreement, defines two types of expropriation. Paragraph (2)(a) calls the first of these *direct expropriation*, "where a covered investment is nationalized or otherwise directly expropriated through formal transfer of title or outright seizure."

---

[40] The obscurity of the politicization of entry barriers to FDI is discussed in Chapter 5, Section 5.6.3.

[41] The RCEP Agreement is discussed in Chapter 7, Section 7.3.2.1.

6.5.4.2   Unilateral Renegotiation

The severity of unilateral renegotiation is seen as being lower than expropriations and nationalisms, because it does not result in the loss of control of FDI operations and/or the loss of the investment. Also, in most cases, even where unilateral renegotiations have resulted in FDIs operating at a loss, the foreign direct investors have, for a range of operational and strategic reasons, chosen to continue to operate their FDI in the host country.

> The RCEP Agreement
> Annex 10B: Expropriation, Paragraphs (2)(b) and (3), of the RCEP Agreement, define a second type of expropriation: "where an action or a series of actions ... has an effect equivalent to direct expropriation without formal transfer of title or outright seizure." Unlike the definition contained in Paragraph (2)(a), which calls the first type *direct expropriation*, Paragraphs (2)(b) and (3) do not name this type of expropriation, but the actions discussed in these paragraphs appear to be referring to various forms of unilateral renegotiation.

The frequency of the use of unilateral renegotiation by host-country governments has, like the use of expropriations and nationalisms, declined since the end of the repudiation phase of post-colonial nationalism—and the exposure to this form of political risk is now low. Also, the use of this form has shifted from being industry specific to being company specific.[42]

6.5.4.3   The Politicization of Administrative Barriers

The politicization of administrative barriers to FDI can have a wide range of severities—from an entity having to cease operations until the host-country government has approved the importation of an essential production line component, to additions to the difficulty and cost of doing business that can result from the absence of established administrative procedures. Compared to the other forms of post-entry FDI political

---

[42] These political-risk specificities are discussed in Sections 6.5.5.1 and 6.5.5.3.

risks, however, all of the administrative-barrier severities are relatively low, and, in most cases, are relatively manageable.[43]

The frequency of the politicization of administrative barriers to FDI is high. Although it is difficult to quantify the frequency of these politicizations, there is abundant anectodical evidence. Senior-level executives at almost every entity engaged in the conduct of FDI can cite numerous incidents where the politicization of a governmental administrative function has added to the difficulty and/or cost of doing business.

6.5.5   Political Risk Specificities

Political risk exposures include: (1) industry-specific political risk, (2) home-country-specific political risk, and (3) company-specific political risk. The distinctions between these three specificities apply to trade, to entry barriers to FDI, and to the post-entry politicized treatment of foreign-funded companies and their FDI operations.

6.5.5.1   Industry-Specific Political Risk

When the political risk exposure of a foreign-funded company is influenced by the industry or industry segment in which it operates, this is called *industry-specific political risk*. Historically, the highest levels of industry-specific political risk to post-entry FDI have been in the oil and mining industries. In some developing countries, FDI in extractive industries continues to have a higher exposure to politicized actions by a host-country government than FDI in other industries.

> Bolivia: Oil and gas companies
>   In 2006, the government of Bolivia announced it had nationalized the country's oil and gas industry, and gave the industry's 10 foreign-funded companies (from six home countries) six months to renegotiate their terms of ownership and operations or face expulsion.

---

[43] Davies. n.d. "International operations: Managing political vulnerability."

In developed countries, industry-specific political risk exposures for FDI most frequently occur in the agriculture, defense, information technology, and social media industries.

6.5.5.2   Home-Country-Specific Political Risk

When the political risk exposure of a foreign-funded company is influenced by its corporate nationality,[44] this is called *home-country-specific political risk*.

Venezuela: AES and Owens Illinois

The relations between the US and Venezuela are contentious and ideologically and politically polarized. Because AES Corporation and Owens Illinois are both US nationals, the expropriation of Owens Illinois and the nationalization of the in-country assets of AES Corporation in Venezuela[45] may have been influenced by home-country-specific political risk.

6.5.5.3   Company-Specific Political Risk

When the politicized action by a host-country government is directed toward a specific foreign-funded company or its operations, this is called *company-specific political risk*. A foreign-funded company's political risk exposure to company-specific political risk may, or may not, be influenced by its behavior and/or reputation in the host country.

Venezuela: Owens Illinois

The expropriation of the operations of Owens Illinois, in 2010, by the government of Venezuela, may have been influenced by company-specific political risk. Following the expropriation, President Hugo Chavez said in a televised speech that the company "has exploited workers for years and has destroyed the

---

[44] Corporate nationality is discussed in Chapter 7, Section 7.1.4.
[45] These actions by the government of Venezuela are discussed in Sections 6.5.3.1 and 6.5.3.2.

environment in [the state of] Trujillo ... and they have taken away the money of Venezuelans."[46] It is possible, however, that the government of Venezuela was in fact (or also) using Owens Illinois as a high-profile whipping boy to motivate compliant behaviors by other foreign-funded companies (including, but not limited to, US foreign-funded companies).

6.5.5.4   Changes in Emphasis

During the repudiation phase of post-colonial nationalism, when the governments of developing countries were targeting FDI in their oil and mining industries, and FDI operations in other extractive industries, the greatest exposure to political risk was to industry-specific actions, with some governments also applying home-country criteria to entities within an industry or industry segment. Since then (with the exception of the actions by the government of Iran, following the Iranian Revolution in 1979, which targeted both trade and FDI, and were largely US home-country specific) political risk exposures for both trade and FDI have included a combination of all three specificities, with an increasing emphasis on company-specific exposures.

This increasing emphasis on company-specific actions, in both trade and FDI, and entry and post-entry barriers to FDI, has been accompanied by a tendency for governments to target a single entity—and, in some cases, a single individual at a single entity. This allows the government to argue that the action was taken in response to the foreign-funded company's behavior, to minimize the possible adverse effects of the action, and to maximize the action's political benefit.

6.5.6   *Socio-Political Risks*

In addition to the forms of political risk exposures discussed in Section 6.5.3, there are socio-political actions that can adversely affect the conduct of international trade, and/or adversely affect the operations

---

[46] Hernandez. n.d. "Venezuela's Chávez Orders Expropriation."

of foreign-funded companies in host countries. Because socio-political actions are not attributable to the politicization of a government's regulatory authority, they do not fall within the definition of political risk. But because socio-political actions can result in adverse effects that are similar to the adverse effects of some political risk exposures, and because in many cases socio-political actions are related to actions (or the absence of actions) by governmental entities, they can be seen as quasi-political risks.

Peru: Las Bambas road-blocking protests

Las Bambas, in Apurimac, Peru, is one of the world's largest copper mines, and is jointly owned by three Chinese state-owned enterprises: MMG Ltd, CNIC Corporation, and CITIC Metal Co Ltd. Since the mine began operations in 2016, protests by community activists over environmental contamination and commercial demands have for extended periods blocked the road between the mine and its export shipping terminal in Matarani. These protests have resulted in the suspension of mining operations for a total of more than 400 days, and the disruption of the exportation of the mine's output to China.

Canada: Covid-19 anti-vaccination protests

In 2022, protests by truck drivers and their sympathizers in Canada, against the government's Covid-19 vaccination requirements, disrupted the supply of parts to a car manufacturing plant in Ontario that is owned and operated by Honda (a Japanese foreign-funded company), which led to the suspension of the plant's production lines.

These Covid-19 anti-vaccination protests also affected the conduct of international trade, by preventing the delivery of parts from suppliers in Canada to General Motors, Ford, Toyota, and other car and truck manufacturing plants in the United States.

Socio-political risks can have a wide range of severities, can have a wide range of frequencies, and can add to the difficulty and/or cost of doing business.

PART III

Facilitating Factors

CHAPTER 7

An Introduction to Instruments and Mechanisms

Contents

7.1   Terms, Concepts, and Definitions

The terms *nation*, *state*, *nation-state*, and *country* are similar in meaning, and all are used in this book—with the choice of term in each case being dependent on context. Of these, the most frequently used term is *country*, because this is the most widely used term in "The General Agreement on Tariffs and Trade" (GATT), other WTO instruments,[1] and non-WTO global instruments that affect the conduct of international trade and FDI.

7.1.1   Nation-State, State, and Nation

In the field of international relations (IR), there is general agreement that the origin of the term *nation-state* is tied to the Peace of Westphalia, and to the development of the concept of sovereignty (which is discussed in Section 7.1.5). There is, however, no generally agreed-upon definition of the term. The declarative theory of statehood says a nation-state has four

---

[1] The GATT and other WTO instruments are discussed in Chapter 8. All references to the GATT that do not specify a year are to GATT 1994 (which includes GATT 1947). This is discussed in Chapter 8, Section 8.4.3.2.

essential characteristics: (1) a defined territory, (2) a permanent population, (3) an established government, and (4) the capacity to engage in relations with other states. The constitutive theory of statehood says there is a single essential criterion: recognition by other states.

In the field of IR, the terms *state* and *nation-state* tend to be used interchangeably. Some intergovernmental instruments[2] (such as the "Charter of the United Nations") use the term *state*, but the most widely used of these two terms is *nation-state*. This usage may be to avoid ambiguity—because some countries use the term *state* when referring to their territorial/political sub-units.[3]

In the fields of IR and international commerce, the use of the term *nation* (and its use in derivative terms such as *national government*, *member nations*, *United Nations*, and *international*) is the same as the term *nation-state*. For example, some WTO instruments, such as the "Agreement Establishing the WTO,"[4] use the terms *nation* and *national* when referring to nation-states; and the terms *nation*, *state*, and *nation-state* are often used interchangeably. The 1967 "ASEAN Declaration" refers to *Member Nations*. The 2008 "ASEAN Charter" refers to *Member States*.[5]

In some fields, including sociology and anthropology, the term *nation* refers to a community of people that shares a common language, culture, ethnicity, descent, and history—such as the Cherokee Nation.[6] In these fields, the term *nation-state* refers to a state where geographical boundaries are coterminous with the national or ethnic identity of its population. These meanings do not apply to the general usage of the terms *nation*, *national*, and *nation-state* in the fields of IR and international commerce.

---

[2] The term *intergovernmental instrument* is discussed in Section 7.3.

[3] These countries include Australia, Austria, Brazil, Germany, India, Malaysia, Mexico, Micronesia, Nigeria, Saint Kitts, Somalia, South Sudan, Sudan, the United States, and Venezuela.

[4] The Agreement Establishing the WTO is discussed in Chapter 8, Section 8.5.

[5] ASEAN is discussed in Chapter 9.

[6] "The Cherokee nation, then, is a distinct community ... The very term *nation* so generally applied to them, means *a people distinct from others*." Chief Justice John Marshal, US Supreme Court, Worcester v. Georgia (1832), page 31 U.S. 519.

7.1.2   Country

In most cases, when the word *country* is used in the GATT, in other WTO instruments, and in non-WTO global instruments that affect the conduct of international trade and/or FDI, it is used as a general term for *state* or *nation-state*.

7.1.2.1   Country Compound Terms

The word *country* is also used in many compound terms. The terms *exporting country* and *importing country* are specific to international trade; *home country* and *host country* are specific to FDI, and can be applied to both individuals and companies; *home country* refers to the nation-state where an individual or a company is a national; and *host country* refers to the country that is the location of a foreign-funded company and its FDI operations.

When referring to an individual or a company, the terms *home country* and *host country* can be used with *national*: *home-country national* or *host-country national*. An individual or entity that is not a host-country national can also be called a *foreign national* or as a *non-national*. Other country compound terms include: *home-* and *host-country government*, *home-* and *host-country courts*, *third country*,[7] *country of origin*,[8] *developed country*, *developing country*, and *least developed country*.

7.1.2.2   Developed and Developing Countries

The terms *developed country* and *developing country*[9] are important classifications in international commerce, because some instruments, such as the GATT and the GATS,[10] allow developing countries preferential treatment

---

[7] The term *third country* is discussed in Chapter 4, Section 4.2.4; and Chapter 12, Section 12.2.4.1.

[8] The term *country of origin* is discussed in Chapter 2, Section 2.4.

[9] In the field of international political economy, and some areas of international relations, the preferred terms are *developed economy* and *developing economy* or *less developed economy*.

[10] The GATT is discussed in Chapter 8. The GATS is discussed in Chapter 8, Sections 8.4.3.2, 8.5.3, and 8.5.3.1.

in countervailing duty investigations,[11] additional time to come into compliance with requirements, greater market access for some products, the more liberal use of safeguards,[12] and access to technical assistance.

The WTO says about two-thirds of the WTO's members are developing countries, but determining which members are developing countries can be problematic, because "there are no WTO definitions of *developed* and *developing* countries. Members announce for themselves whether they are *developed* or *developing* countries."[13] The absence of WTO definitions of *developed* and *developing* countries can also be problematic, because this allows the governments of developed countries to use their own criteria when deciding which countries they will treat as developing and least developed countries.

The US: List of developing countries

The Office of the US Trade Representative (USTR) maintains a "list of countries designated as developing or least-developed under U.S. countervailing duty laws," which receive "differential treatment."[14] In February 2020, the USTR announced that it had removed more than 20 countries from the list.[15]

7.1.2.3   Least Developed Countries

In 1971, the United Nations Conference on Trade and Development (UNCTAD) created a subcategory of developing countries, which it called *least developed countries* (LDCs), which UNCTAD defines as "States that are deemed highly disadvantaged in their development process, for structural, historical and also geographical reasons."[16] UNCTAD provides a list of LDCs, which it reviews every three years. This list includes

---

[11] Countervailing duty investigations are discussed in Chapter 4, Section 4.3.4.2.

[12] Safeguards are discussed in Chapter 3, Section 3.3.3.

[13] "Who are the developing countries in the WTO?"

[14] USTR Updates List of Developing and Least-Developed Countries Under U.S. CVD Law.

[15] U.S. Federal Register. n.d. "Designations of Developing and Least-Developed Countries Under the Countervailing Duty Law."

[16] "UN recognition of the least developed countries."

about 50 countries, which UNCTAD says comprise about 880 million people, 12 percent of the world's population, and account for less than 2 percent of world GDP and about 1 percent of world trade. The WTO says it recognizes as LDCs those countries that have been designated by UNCTAD.[17] Because LDCs are a subcategory of developing countries, references in this book to developing countries include LDCs.

The term *North* is sometimes used as a collective noun synecdoche for all developed countries; the term *South* is sometimes used as a collective noun synecdoche for all developing countries and least developed countries.

7.1.3   Customs Territories

The GATT uses the terms *country, customs territory, separate customs territory,* and *single customs territory.* Article XXIV, 2, of the GATT says: "a customs territory shall be understood to mean any territory with respect to which separate tariffs or other regulations of commerce are maintained for a substantial part of the trade of such territory with other territories." Article XXXIII of the GATT, and Article XII of the "Marrakesh Agreement" (MA),[18] refer to a separate customs territory (SCT)[19] as an entity "possessing full autonomy in the conduct of its external commercial relations." Because these definitions apply to countries, the GATT uses the terms *country* and *customs territory* interchangeably.[20]

There are three types of separate customs territories: (1) customs unions, which include several or many nationstates, (2) territories of nation-states, and (3) independent territories.

Article XXIV, paragraph 8(a), of the GATT says: "A customs union shall be understood to mean the substitution of a single customs territory for two or more customs territories."[21] A customs union (CU) can,

---

[17] "Understanding the WTO: The organization: Least-Developed Countries."

[18] The MA is discussed in Chapter 8, Section 8.5. The definition and use of the term *separate customs territory* in Article XII of the MA were borrowed from Article XXXIII of the GATT.

[19] This book uses the initialism SCT to mean *separate customs territory,* as distinct from *single customs territory.* SCTs are discussed in Chapter 8, Section 8.5.2.1.

[20] The exception is China, which includes Hong Kong, which is a separate customs territory.

[21] Customs unions are discussed in Chapter 9, Section 9.4.

therefore, be referred to as a *single customs territory*. Because CUs possess full autonomy in the conduct of their external commercial relations, they are also called *separate customs territories* (SCTs).

The US: SCTs

American Samoa, Guam, Northern Mariana Islands, US Minor Outlaying Islands, and the US Virgin Islands are SCTs that are territories of the United States.

The WTO: SCT members

There are four SCTs that are members of the WTO: the European Union (1995), Hong Kong (1995), Macao (1995), and Taiwan (2002).[22]

SCTs in WTO plurilateral agreements

The "Agreement on Government Procurement" (GPA), which is a WTO plurilateral agreement,[23] includes participation by 48 WTO members. These include Hong Kong and Taiwan, which are SCTs, but do not include China, which is a nation-state and a GPA observer.

Because Article XXXIII of the GATT and Article XII of the "Marrakesh Agreement" provide that membership in the WTO is open to nation-states and separate customs territories, in the conduct of international commercial relations all references to countries include SCTs; references to nationals of nation-states include nationals or residents of separate customs territories; and many of the rights and duties of states also apply to SCTs.

7.1.4 Corporate Nationality

In most cases, determining the nationality of an individual who is a foreign direct investor is not difficult, because his or her nationality is defined by their citizenship. Determining the nationality of a company or

---

[22] Membership of SCTs in the WTO is discussed in Chapter 8, Section 8.5.2.1.

[23] WTO plurilateral agreements are discussed in Chapter 8, Section 8.4.3.3.

other commercial entity, which is referred to as *corporate nationality*, can be more problematic—because there is no generally agreed-upon set of criteria for corporate nationality.

The criteria that define corporate nationality are set by the government of each host country. In some cases, different departments of a national government (such as the US Treasury and the US Department of Commerce) use different criteria for determining corporate nationality. The most widely used criteria are: (1) the nation-state within which a company is incorporated, (2) the nationality of a company's principal shareholders, (3) the nationality of the company's major sources of funding, (4) the nation-state within which the company has its principal administrative offices, and (5) the nation-state within which the company has its principal operations.

If the nationality of an entity's principal shareholder(s) is different from the entity's country of incorporation, the entity can be called a *foreign corporation*, *foreign-owned corporation*, *foreign-funded corporation*, or *non-national corporation*—or any of these terms where the word *company*, *enterprise*, or *entity* is used in place of the word *corporation*. The governments in different countries, however, use a range of different terms when referring to these corporations, companies, or entities.

The US: Affiliates

In the United States, if a company's incorporation is domestic and the nationality of its principal shareholder(s) is foreign (such as American Honda Motor Co., Inc.,[24] which is incorporated in the US and has a Japanese company as its principal shareholder), the company is called a *US affiliate* or a *US affiliate of a foreign company*. If the nationality of a company's principal shareholders is domestic and its incorporation is foreign (such as Apple Operations International, which is incorporated in Ireland and has a US company as its principal shareholder), the company is called a *foreign affiliate* or a *foreign affiliate of a US parent company*.

---

[24] AHM is discussed in Chapter 5, Section 5.2.2.

7.1.5   Sovereignty

The concept of sovereignty has two dimensions:

1. The internal dimension provides that a national government has authority over everything that occurs within the territorial borders of its nation-state—and has the sole and absolute right to exercise this authority.
2. The external dimension provides that a national government has the right to represent its nation-state in relations with other nation-states—and the duty not to intervene in the internal affairs of other nation-states.

7.1.5.1   The Origin of the Concept

The term *sovereignty* was first defined by the French philosopher Jean Bodin. In "De la république," written in 1576, Bodin argued that the only way to ensure order in society was for the ruled and the rulers to be integrated into a single body, and for this body to have sole and absolute authority within a territory. Bodin called this concept *souveraineté*.

The concept of sovereignty, as it is currently applied in the field of international relations, originated in Europe in the 17th century. Before 1648, most states in Europe were part of a complicated system that divided political authority between local rulers (the princes and kings) and the Pope, who was head of the Catholic Church and the Holy Roman Empire. In most cases, the local rulers exercised authority over secular areas; the Catholic Church exercised authority over religious and ecclesiastical issues.[25] It was not unusual, however, for local princes and kings to claim they had authority over the appointment of clergy and other religious matters; and in most states the Church controlled land that it taxed and defended, and was involved in other secular matters. These imbricate jurisdictions resulted in competing claims of authority, and led

---

[25] Religious issues include theological beliefs and ideology. Ecclesiastical issues include the appointment of clergy and the administration of the church and its land and buildings.

to numerous wars between states and the Holy Roman Empire. The last of these wars ended with the Peace of Westphalia in 1648.

7.1.5.2   The Peace of Westphalia

The Peace of Westphalia[26] was a series of treaties. These treaties were not uniform; they did not define a new system; and they did not refer to the concept of sovereignty. But the Westphalia treaties are seen as collectively having originated the use of the concept of sovereignty—and, for several reasons, as having established the principles of sovereignty in the conduct of international relations.

First, some of the Westphalia treaties (especially those with the Netherlands and Switzerland) granted rulers of a territory supreme and sole authority over all matters (both temporal and religious) within their borders. This established the internal dimension of sovereignty. Second, some of the treaties (especially those with the German states) granted individual states the right to form alliances with states outside the Holy Roman Empire. This established the external characteristic of sovereignty relating to the authority of national governments in the conduct of international relations. Third, the treaties denied the Holy Roman Empire the power to intervene in the internal affairs of a nation-state. This established the external characteristic of sovereignty relating to non-intervention in the internal affairs of other states. And finally, because the Westphalia treaties removed religion as a criterion for the division of authority, the only defining characteristic that remained was territory. This established the principle that the concept of sovereignty relates solely to a nation-state's geographical territory.

7.1.5.3   The Partial Surrender of Sovereignty

A principal characteristic of the concept of sovereignty that emerged from the Westphalia treaties, which ended the division of sovereignty between local rulers and the Pope, was that sovereignty is not divisible. But when the government of a nation-state enters into a treaty or agreement[27] with

---

[26] Westphalia was a province in what is now Germany.
[27] Treaties and agreements are discussed in Section 7.3.1.

one or more other nation-states, and agrees to cede its absolute authority and control over something that falls under either the internal or external dimensions of sovereignty (or falls under both of these dimensions), it can be seen as engaging in the division of some aspects of their nation-state's sovereignty—and voluntarily surrendering part of its sovereignty.

For example, because every member of the WTO has ratified the GATT, and because the national treatment clause contained in Article III of the GATT[28] mandates the treatment that must be afforded to products that have been imported from the customs territories of other members, all WTO members have surrendered their sovereign authority to determine how they will treat imported products within the territorial borders of their nation-state. Also, because nation-states that become members of a customs union[29] must surrender all of the trade-related parts of their sovereignty, "it is impossible to envisage a common market or economic union in which member states have not partially ceded sovereignty."[30]

In his "Essay on Sovereignty, December 1835," James Madison argued: "if two States, could thus incorporate themselves into one, by a mutual surrender of the entire sovereignty of each; why might not a partial incorporation, by a partial surrender of sovereignty, be equally practicable ... and if this could be done, by two States, why not by twenty or more," and that "a division of sovereignty, is, in fact illustrated by the exchange of sovereign rights often involved in Treaties between Independent Nations."[31]

7.1.6 *Preferential Trade Agreements*

When an importing country reduces a customs tariff, NTB, or other barrier to trade on a product category from an exporting country, the GATT refers to this as granting the exporting country "preferences in respect of import duties or charges."[32] The term *preference* and its derivatives are widely used in the field of international commerce. For example, the

---

[28] The national treatment clause is discussed in Chapter 8, Section 8.4.2.
[29] Customs unions are discussed in Chapter 9, Section 9.4.
[30] Oppong. n.d. *Legal Aspects of Economic Integration in Africa*, p. 89.
[31] Madison. n.d. "Essay on Sovereignty, December 1835."
[32] GATT, Article I, Paragraph 2.

terms *preference, preferential, preferential treatment, preferential arrange-ments,* and *preferential rate* appear a total of 54 times in the GATT; and the common internal tariffs in free trade areas (FTAs) are called *prefer-ential tariffs.*[33] Because the provisions contained in regional and bilateral trade agreements[34] provide trade preferences to the countries that are par-ties to these instruments—these instruments are called *preferential trade agreements (PTAs).* PTAs can be either regional PTAs or bilateral PTAs.

7.1.6.1   PTAs and Initialism Ambiguity

The initialism PTA is generally used to mean *preferential trade agree-ment.* But the WTO uses this initialism when referring to *preferential trade arrangements,* which are the unilateral trade preferences that are listed in the WTO's PTA Database. Also, because trade preferences are the primary means for reducing or eliminating trade barriers between the members of regional trade blocks (RTBs),[35] which include free trade areas[36] and customs unions, RTBs are sometimes called *preferential trade areas*—using the initialism PTA. To avoid the ambiguity that can result from these different usages of the initialism, this book uses PTA to mean *preferential trade agreement,* and uses the initialisms RTB, FTA, or CU when referring to a regional trade block, free trade area, or customs union that has been created by a PTA.

7.1.6.2   WTO Notification

Article XXIV, paragraph 7.(a) of the GATT says when WTO members are entering into a PTA that will create an FTA or CU, they must notify the WTO regarding their intention, and provide it with related informa-tion. About 350 PTAs have been notified to the WTO and have entered into force.

---

[33] Preferential tariffs are discussed in Chapter 2, Section 2.1.6; and Chapter 9, Section 9.3.3.1.
[34] Regional and bilateral trade agreements are discussed in Chapter 9.
[35] Regional trade blocks are discussed in Chapter 9, Section 9.2.
[36] Free trade areas are discussed in Chapter 9, Sections 9.2.4 and 9.3.

7.2   Intergovernmental Factors

The use of the term *intergovernmental factor*, in this book, refers to an instrument and/or mechanism that affects the conduct of international commerce—that is created and controlled by the governments of two or more countries[37] for the primary purpose of achieving mutually beneficial economic goals.

Intergovernmental factors include:

- "The General Agreement on Tariffs and Trade;"
- World Trade Organization[38];
- European Union, the ASEAN Free Trade Area, the "United States-Mexico-Canada Agreement," and the Regional Comprehensive Economic Partnership[39];
- Hundreds of bilateral trade and investment agreements, and bilateral free trade areas[40]; and
- Instruments and mechanisms for the harmonization of laws and mechanisms for the settlement of international commercial disputes, which include the International Center for the Settlement of Investment Disputes (ICSID) and the Dispute Settlement Body of the WTO.[41]

7.2.1   The Effects of the Intergovernmental Factors

The trade and investment barriers discussed in Chapters 2 through 6, which are applied by the governments of single nation-states, restrict and/or regulate the conduct of international trade and/or FDI. The intergovernmental factors discussed in this chapter, and in Chapters 8

---

[37] In the field of international commerce, references to countries or nation-states include separate customs territories. This is discussed in Section 7.1.3.
[38] The GATT and the WTO are discussed in Chapter 8.
[39] The EU, the ASEAN Free Trade Area, the USMCA, the RCEP, and other regional intergovernmental factors are discussed in Chapter 9.
[40] Bilateral instruments and mechanisms are discussed in Chapter 9, Section 9.5.
[41] The harmonization of laws is discussed in Chapter 11. The settlement of international commercial disputes is discussed in Chapter 12.

through 12 (together with the non-governmental factors discussed in Chapters 10 through 12), facilitate the conduct of international trade and FDI.

The intergovernmental facilitating factors:

- Reduce or eliminate barriers to international trade and foreign investment;
- Provide the conceptual, structural, and legal parameters that govern or influence the policies, laws, regulations, decisions, and actions of single nation-states;
- Govern or influence how the governments of single nation-states treat companies engaged in the practice of international trade and/or FDI;
- Establish and implement product, process, and behavioral standards that facilitate the conduct of international commerce;
- Harmonize the conflict of laws that affect the conduct of international commerce; and
- Facilitate the settlement of international commercial disputes.

7.2.2   Primary Classifications

All intergovernmental factors can be classified as either instruments or mechanisms.

- Intergovernmental instruments are discussed in Section 7.3.
- Intergovernmental mechanisms are discussed in Section 7.4.
- Intergovernmental instruments and mechanisms are discussed in Sections 7.5 and 7.6.

Intergovernmental instruments and mechanisms can be classified by their number of participants, and/or by their geographical scope. When applied to an instrument and/or mechanism:

- The term *unilateral* indicates participation in an instrument (such as a declaration, or the unilateral trade preferences that are listed in the WTO's PTA Database) by a single nation-state.

- The term *bilateral* indicates participation in an instrument or mechanism by two nation-states. Bilateral instruments and mechanisms are discussed in Chapter 9, Section 9.5.
- The term *multilateral* indicates participation in an instrument or mechanism by three or more nation-states. An exception to this is the *sui generis* usage and meaning of this term within the WTO.[42]
- The term *global* refers to an instrument or mechanism that includes participation by countries from all parts of the world, to an instrument and its provisions that apply to or in all parts of the world, and to a mechanism and its operational functions that are present in and/or that affect all parts of the world. Global instruments and mechanisms are discussed in Section 7.7 of this chapter, and in Chapter 8.
- The term *region* (or *regional*) refers to a geographical area or sub-area of the world that has definable characteristics. Regional instruments and mechanisms are discussed in Chapter 9.

When applied to intergovernmental instruments and mechanisms, the terms *global* and *regional* can refer to geographical participation, geographical scope, and/or to geographical areas of interest, application, or influence.[43]

7.3   Intergovernmental Instruments

The term *instrument* is a technical term that covers all written agreements. Intergovernmental instruments are written agreements between nation-states—which allow governments to state and agree to terms and conditions that govern the conduct of international relations. In the conduct of international commerce, intergovernmental instruments:

---

[42] This is discussed in Chapter 8, Section 8.4.3.3.

[43] Exceptions to this usage of the term *regional* are discussed in Chapter 9, Section 9.2.3.

- Provide the legal and operational framework for the conduct of international commerce;
- Contain the concepts, principles, rules, and requirements that regulate the behavior of nationstates related to the conduct of international commerce;
- Provide nation-states with the means to establish, record, and preserve their rights and duties with other nation-states related to the conduct of international commerce;
- Provide nation-states with the means, and the legal and procedural frameworks, for the creation and operation of international mechanisms;
- Provide product, process, and behavioral standards;
- Facilitate transparency in the conduct of international commerce.[44]

7.3.1 Treaties and Agreements

In the field of international relations, intergovernmental instruments are divided into two primary categories: agreements[45] and treaties.

- The agreements category includes five subcategories: *agreements*, *declarations*, *memoranda of understanding* (MOUs), *modus vivendi*, and *communiqués*.[46]
- The treaties category includes six subcategories: *treaties*, *charters*, *conventions*, *covenants*, *statutes*, and *protocols*.

Each of the instruments from these two sets of subcategories has particular applications. There are, however, no rules governing which type of instrument must be used in a particular situation. Also, the "United Nations Treaty Handbook" says that "the title and form of a document ... are less important than its content in determining whether

---

[44] Transparency is discussed in Chapter 6, Section 6.4.2.

[45] The UN Vienna Convention refers to the agreements category as *international agreements*.

[46] Information concerning treaty and agreement categories can be found in the UN Treaty Reference Guide and the "UN Treaty Handbook."

it is a treaty or international agreement,"[47] which allows nation-states considerable latitude when choosing the operative term to use in the title of an instrument. Despite this allowance for latitude, terms from the treaties category are usually reserved for titles of instruments that have a high level of importance—although there are many exceptions to this general rule. For example, the title of the GATT instrument uses the term *agreement*, but this instrument has a high level of importance.[48]

Treaties and other instruments in the treaties category are more often used as global and multilateral instruments. Agreements and other instruments in the agreements category are more often used as regional and bilateral instruments. The titles of subordinate instruments of constitutional treaties frequently use one of the terms from the agreements category, even if the subordinate instrument requires ratification. This is done to indicate that the instrument is a subordinate instrument of a constitutional treaty.

7.3.2   Acceptance Procedures

The most significant difference between treaties and agreements relates to their acceptance procedures. The term *acceptance* or *acceptance procedure* refers to the decisions and actions that must be taken by a nation-state for it to become a party to an instrument.

As a general rule, agreements do not require ratification; treaties require ratification. As with the use of the terms *agreement* and *treaty* in the titles of instruments, there are many exceptions and inconsistencies to this general rule. These exceptions and inconsistencies are discussed in Section 7.3.2.5.

7.3.2.1   Ratification

In most cases, acceptance for an instrument in the treaties category that has not entered into force is a two-step process. The first step is called *simple signature*—which is not binding, but indicates a nation-state's intention to commit to the treaty.

---

[47] "UN Treaty Handbook," Section 5.3.2, Form.
[48] The reason for the choice of the term *agreement* in the title of the GATT is discussed in Chapter 8, Section 8.2.3.1.

The second step is called *ratification*—which refers to the adoption of a resolution by the government of a nation-state that demonstrates "its willingness to undertake the legal rights and obligations contained in the treaty."[49] Ratification also requires that treaty and approval documents be exchanged (in the case of bilateral treaties) or deposited with the designated depository (in the case of multilateral treaties).

The GCC—Singapore FTA

In 2008, the member governments of the Gulf Cooperation Council (GCC)[50] signed a free trade agreement with Singapore. Because of the delayed ratification by one GCC member, the agreement did not enter into force until 2012.

The RCEP

The Regional Comprehensive Economic Partnership (RCEP), which includes 15 members (the 10 members of ASEAN plus 5 other members),[51] was created by the "Regional Comprehensive Economic Partnership Agreement" (RCEP Agreement), which entered into force on January 1, 2022. Paragraph (1) of Article 20.6: Entry into Force, states that "This Agreement shall be subject to ratification, acceptance, or approval by each signatory State in accordance with its applicable legal procedures. The instruments of ratification, acceptance, or approval of a signatory State shall be deposited with the Depository."

7.3.2.2   Entry-Into-Force Thresholds

The acceptance requirements contained in most multilateral treaties include a threshold, which requires that a minimum number of states ratify the treaty, and deposit their approval instruments, before the treaty enters into force.

---

[49] "UN Treaty Handbook," Section 3.3.1, Introduction.
[50] The GCC is discussed in Chapter 9, Sections 9.1.1 and 9.4.2.
[51] The members of the RCEP are: Australia, Brunei, Cambodia, China, Indonesia, Japan, South Korea, Laos, Malaysia, Myanmar, New Zealand, the Philippines, Singapore, Thailand, and Vietnam.

GATT 1947

Article XXVI, Acceptance, Entry into Force and Registration, of GATT 1947, required that for the instrument to enter into force it must be accepted by governments that "account for 85 per centum of the total external trade" of the countries participating in the process.[52]

RCEP

Paragraph (2) of Article 20.6: Entry into Force, of the RCEP Agreement, states that "This Agreement shall enter into force ... 60 days after the date on which at least six signatory States which are Members of ASEAN and three signatory States other than Member States of ASEAN have deposited their instruments of ratification, acceptance, or approval with the Depository."

The term *ratification* is sometimes used as a general term when referring to either ratification or accession.

7.3.2.3 Accession

In most cases, the acceptance procedure for an instrument that has entered into force is called *accession*. The "UN Treaty Handbook" says that "Accession has the same legal effect as ratification."[53] The requirements for accession are the same as for ratification, except that accession is not preceded by simple signature.

Russia: Accession to membership in the WTO

In December 2011, after 18 years of negotiations, the members of the WTO agreed to admit the Russian Federation to full membership. Russia's "Protocol of Accession," the GATT, and about 60 other WTO instruments were ratified by the State Duma on July 10, 2012, and by the Federal Council of Russia on July 18.[54] On July 21, "President Vladimir Putin signed into

---

[52] The GATT 1947 entry-into-force threshold is discussed in Chapter 8, Section 8.2.3.1.

[53] "UN Treaty Handbook," Section 3.3.4, Accession.

[54] The State Duma and the Federal Council of Russia are the lower and upper houses of Russia's parliament: the Federal Assembly of Russia.

law Parliamentary legislation bringing Russia's trading laws and regulations into compliance with the international standards set under the WTO."[55] The Russian Federation's instruments and approval documents were deposited with the United Nations Secretariat in New York, and its membership became effective on August 22, 2012.[56]

If a nation-state is one of the founding signatories to a treaty that requires ratification, or becomes a signatory to the treaty before it enters into force, and approves the treaty after it has entered into force, the action of approving the treaty is called ratification, not accession.

7.3.2.4   Definitive Signature

Subject to the exceptions covered in Section 7.3.2.5, the acceptance procedure for instruments in the agreements category does not require ratification or accession. For these instruments, "states can express their consent to be legally bound solely upon signature"[57]—using a single-step procedure called *definitive signature*. Definitive signature requires that an instrument be signed by a person who holds full powers. The term *full powers* refers to the head of state, the head of government, or the minister of foreign affairs of a nation-state—or a person who has been given full powers by a nation-state to represent it on all matters related to a particular treaty or agreement.

7.3.2.5   Exceptions and Inconsistencies

As noted in Sections 7.3.2 and 7.3.2.4, as a general rule instruments in the agreements category do not require ratification, instruments in the treaties category require ratification—but there are exceptions to this generalization. This is because an instrument's acceptance procedure is not governed by the term contained in the instrument's title, but by the terms contained in its acceptance provisions—which are usually found

---

[55] Press release, Russia's WTO accession ratification.
[56] The Russian Federation became the 156th member of the WTO.
[57] "UN Treaty Handbook," Section 3.1.4, Definitive signature.

near the end of the instrument under the heading *acceptance*. If there is an inconsistency between the term used in the title of an instrument and the terms contained in its acceptance provisions, the instrument's acceptance is governed by the procedure contained in its acceptance provisions.

The Agreement Establishing the WTO

The "Agreement Establishing the WTO" has the word *agreement* in its title. But this agreement requires ratification, because Article XII: Accession (which governs new membership in the WTO) provides that "any state or separate customs territory possessing full autonomy in the conduct of its external commercial relations ... may accede to this agreement."

RCEP Agreement

The RCEP Agreement has the word *agreement* in its title. But this agreement requires ratification, because Paragraph (1) of Article 20.6: Entry into Force of the agreement provides that "This Agreement shall be subject to ratification, acceptance, or approval by each signatory State in accordance with its applicable legal procedures."

7.4 Intergovernmental Mechanisms

Intergovernmental mechanisms are created and maintained by the governments of two or more nation-states. The term *mechanism* is a technical term that covers a range of functional and organizational entities.

7.4.1 The Effects of Intergovernmental Mechanisms

In the field of international relations, intergovernmental mechanisms allow nation-states to implement the provisions contained in intergovernmental instruments, and to achieve intergovernmental policy, strategic, and operational goals. In the conduct of international commerce, intergovernmental mechanisms:

- Provide the organizational, operational, and administrative structures and systems that are used to implement the concepts, principles, and requirements contained in intergovernmental instruments.

- Provide forums that facilitate the proposal, deliberation, discussion, drafting, development, and adoption of amendments to existing intergovernmental instruments, and the creation of new intergovernmental instruments.
- Influence the decisions, actions, and behaviors of nation-states related to the regulation of international trade and foreign direct investment—and related to the treatment of commercial entities.
- Provide the organizational, operational, and administrative structures and systems that facilitate the development and propagation of international standards and the settlement of international commercial disputes.
- Facilitate transparency in the conduct of international trade and FDI.

7.4.2   Organizational Mechanisms

An organizational mechanism is an institutional entity that has a secretariat, an administrative and operational structure, officers, employees, and physical facilities.

Organizational mechanisms that facilitate the conduct of international relations include:

- United Nations (UN) organization
- World Health Organization (WHO)
- International Court of Justice (ICJ) (which is commonly called the *World Court*)
- Association of Southeast Asian Nations (ASEAN)
- Shanghai Cooperation Organization (SCO)

Organizational mechanisms that facilitate the conduct of international trade and/or FDI include:

- World Trade Organization
- World Customs Organization (WCO)
- World Intellectual Property Organization (WIPO)
- European Union

- ASEAN Free Trade Area
- International Center for the Settlement of Investment Disputes
- United Nations Commission on International Trade Law (UNCITRAL)
- International Institute for the Unification of Private Law (UNIDROIT)
- Hague Conference on Private International Law (HCCH)

7.4.3 Functional Mechanisms

A functional mechanism is an operational entity that performs a specific task or function. Functional mechanisms that facilitate the conduct of international relations include:

- Security Council of the United Nations
- Six-Party Talks
- MOUDC (the Memorandum of Understanding on Drug Control), which is a subregional multilateral operational entity that was created to fight the production, trafficking, and use of drugs in the Greater Mekong Subregion

Functional mechanisms that facilitate the conduct of international trade and/or FDI include:

- MFN provision of the GATT
- WTOs multilateral trade negotiations
- WTO Dispute Settlement Body
- The free trade area created by the "United States, Mexico, Canada Agreement" (USMCA)
- Dozens of other multilateral free trade areas[58]
- The free trade area created by the "Canada–EU Comprehensive Economic and Trade Agreement" (CETA)[59] and hundreds of other bilateral free trade areas[60]

---

[58] Multilateral free trade areas are discussed in Chapter 9, Section 9.3.

[59] The CETA is discussed in Chapter 3, Section 3.3.2.2; and in Chapter 9, Section 9.4.3.

[60] Bilateral free trade areas are discussed in Chapter 9, Section 9.5.

7.4.3.1   Functional Mechanisms and Logistical Support

Functional mechanisms are dependent on organizational mechanisms for logistical support. For example, the MFN provision of the GATT,[61] the WTO's multilateral trade negotiations,[62] and the WTO's Dispute Settlement Body[63] are functional mechanisms that are operational sub-units of the WTO—and the WTO organizational mechanism provides logistical support for each of these functional mechanisms.[64] The logistical support for other functional mechanisms, such as bilateral free trade areas, is provided by the operational sub-units of the national governments that are parties to the instrument that has created the mechanism—which, in most cases, are those governments' departments or agencies.

7.4.3.2   The Evolution of Functional Mechanisms

In some cases, functional mechanisms evolve and become organizational mechanisms. For example, the Hague Conference on Private International Law (HCCH) was created as a functional mechanism in 1893, and in 1955 became an intergovernmental organization.[65] The Shanghai Five Mechanism was created as a functional mechanism in 1996, and in 2001 became the Shanghai Cooperation Organization.

7.5   Symbiotic Relationships

There are several essential symbiotic relationships between multilateral intergovernmental instruments and multilateral intergovernmental mechanisms.

1. Instruments create mechanisms. The "Agreement Establishing the WTO" created the WTO.[66] Article 18 (11) of the RCEP

---

[61] The MFN provision of the GATT is discussed in Chapter 8, Section 8.4.1.

[62] The WTO's multilateral trade negotiations are discussed in Chapter 8, Section 8.4.3.

[63] The WTO Dispute Settlement Body is discussed in Chapter 12, Section 12.4.

[64] The term *logistical support* covers a wide range of facilities and functions, which can include offices and office equipment, administrative services, and staff.

[65] The HCCH is discussed in Chapter 11, Section 11.3.2.

[66] The Agreement Establishing the WTO is discussed in Chapter 8, Sections 8.4.3.2 and 8.5.

Agreement[67] created the RCEP Secretariat. The "Treaty on the Eurasian Economic Commission," which came into effect in 2012, created the Eurasian Economic Commission (EEC) as the secretariat of the Eurasian Customs Union (EACU) and of its successor organization, the Eurasian Economic Union (EAEU).[68]

2. Instruments provide the concepts, principles, and legal parameters that govern the conduct of international commerce—and that govern the administration and operations of mechanisms. The "Agreement Establishing the WTO"; the GATT 1994, GATS, TRIPS, and TRIMs instruments;[69] the "Agreement on Rules of Origin";[70] and other WTO instruments provide concepts, principles, rules, requirements, and legal parameters that govern the conduct of international commerce. These instruments also govern the administration and operations of the WTO and its subsidiary bodies. The USMCA instrument[71] provides the concepts, principles, and legal parameters that govern the conduct of international commerce between the United States, Mexico, and Canada.

3. Mechanisms facilitate the amendment of existing instruments. The WTO provides a forum for the proposal, deliberation, discussion, drafting, and adoption of amendments to the GATT instrument and other WTO instruments. The NAFTA's functional mechanisms facilitated the negotiations that resulted in amendments to the NAFTA instrument, which included changing the name of the instrument to the "United States, Mexico, Canada Agreement" (USMCA).

4. Mechanisms facilitate the creation of new instruments. The WTO provides a forum for the proposal, deliberation, discussion, drafting, and adoption of new global intergovernmental instruments that facilitate the conduct of international commerce. The African Union (AU), Session of Assembly of Heads of State and Government, in Addis Ababa, Ethiopia, in January 2012, adopted a decision to establish an African Continental Free Trade Area (AfCFTA) to

---

[67] The RCEP Agreement is discussed in Section 7.3.2.1.

[68] The EEC, the EACU and the EAEU are discussed in Chapter 9, Section 9.4.2.

[69] These instruments are discussed in Chapter 8, Sections 8.4.3.2 and 8.5.3.

[70] The Agreement on Rules of Origin is discussed in Chapter 2, Section 2.4.2.

[71] The USMCA instrument is discussed in Chapter 9, Section 9.2.1.1.

"promote socio-economic growth and development."[72] At the AU meeting in Kigali, Rwanda, in March 2018, 44 of the AU's member states signed the "Agreement Establishing the African Continental Free Trade Area" (AfCFTA Agreement),[73] which entered into force in May 2019. The AfCFTA,[74] in terms of the number of member states, is the world's largest FTA.

7.6   Relative Visibility and Importance

Intergovernmental instruments are relatively obscure, whereas intergovernmental mechanisms are relatively visible. For example, there are frequent references in the media to the WTO, and we often see media images of national leaders attending meetings of intergovernmental organizations. But we rarely see references in the media to the GATT, GATS, TRIPS, or TRIMs instruments, or to other WTO instruments, and we only occasionally see references to trade and investment treaties that have been signed and later ratified by national governments.

This relative visibility does not reflect the relative importance of intergovernmental instruments and mechanisms. Intergovernmental mechanisms provide the organizational and operational factors that facilitate the conduct of international trade and FDI. It is the relatively obscure intergovernmental instruments, however, that provide the legal and operational framework—and prescribe the concepts, principles, rules, and requirements—that govern and facilitate the conduct of international trade and FDI.

7.7   Non-WTO Global Instruments and Mechanisms

As discussed in Chapter 8, Section 8.1, the predominant instruments that facilitate the conduct of international trade and FDI are "The General Agreement on Tariffs and Trade" and other WTO instruments; the predominant facilitating mechanism is the WTO. But the conduct of

---

[72] African Union, The African Continental Free Trade Area website.
[73] The AfCFTA Agreement was subsequently signed by another 10 AU members.
[74] The AfCFTA is discussed in Chapter 9, Section 9.3.1.

international trade and FDI is also facilitated by non-WTO global instruments and mechanisms—and by regional and bilateral instruments and mechanisms.

Non-WTO global instruments and mechanisms are discussed in this section. Regional and bilateral instruments and mechanisms are discussed in Chapter 9.

7.7.1 Non-WTO Global Instruments

Non-WTO global intergovernmental instruments that facilitate the conduct of international trade and/or FDI include:

- United Nations Set of Principles and Rules on Competition
- Convention Establishing the World Intellectual Property Organization
- Convention on the Settlement of Investment Disputes between States and Nationals of Other the States (the ICSID Convention)
- Convention establishing a Customs Co-operation Council
- Convention on the Valuation of Goods for Customs Purposes
- Customs Convention on the International Transit of Goods (the ITI Convention)
- International Convention on the Simplification and Harmonization of Customs Procedures (the Kyoto Convention[75])
- International Convention on the Harmonized Commodity Description and Coding System (the HS Convention)
- United Nations Convention on Contracts for the International Sale of Goods
- Convention on the Recognition and Enforcement of Foreign Arbitral Awards
- Convention on Stolen or Illegally Exported Cultural Objects
- Convention on International Interests in Mobile Equipment

---

[75] This instrument is distinct from the Kyoto Protocol, which is the "United Nations Framework Convention on Climate Change."

- Convention on the Service Abroad of Judicial and Extrajudicial Documents in Civil or Commercial Matters
- Convention on the Taking of Evidence Abroad in Civil or Commercial Matters

The first instrument on the above list, "UN Set of Principles and Rules on Competition," was created by the United Nations Conference on Restrictive Business Practices, under the auspices of the United Nations Conference on Trade and Development (UNCTAD), between 1978 and 1980. It was adopted by the General Assembly of the United Nations in 1980, and has since been reviewed every five years. This set of principles and rules influences the policies, laws, and regulations that are used by nation-states relating to competition, which can facilitate the FDI operations of foreign-funded companies.

The second and third instruments on the list were created, respectively, by the World Intellectual Property Organization and the International Center for the Settlement of Investment Disputes. The fourth instrument on the list was created by the Customs Co-operation Council, which in 1995 became the World Customs Organization (WCO). The next four instruments on the list were created by the WCO. The last four instruments on the list are discussed in Chapter 11, Section 11.3.1.

7.7.2   Non-WTO Global Mechanisms

Non-WTO global intergovernmental mechanisms that facilitate the conduct of international trade and/or FDI include:

- United Nations Conference on Trade and Development, and its Program on Transnational Corporations
- United Nations International Trade Center
- Organization for Economic Cooperation and Development (OECD)
- World Intellectual Property Organization
- World Customs Organization

- United Nations Commission for International Trade and Law (UNCITRAL)
- International Institute for the Unification of Private Law (UNIDROIT)
- Hague Conference on Private International Law (HCCH)
- International Center for the Settlement of Investment Disputes

The last three mechanisms on this list are discussed in Chapter 11, Section 11.3.2.

The ICSID mechanism is discussed in Chapter 12, Section 12.2.5.2.

CHAPTER 8

The GATT and the WTO

Contents

8.1   Introduction

The predominant instruments that facilitate the conduct of international trade and FDI are "The General Agreement on Tariffs and Trade" (GATT)[1] and other WTO instruments.[2] The predominant facilitating mechanism is the WTO. The concepts, principles, rules, requirements, legal frameworks, and operational provisions contained in the GATT and other WTO instruments, and the principles employed by the WTO functional mechanisms,[3] are reflected in hundreds of regional and bilateral instruments and mechanisms that facilitate the conduct of international trade and/or FDI.

---

[1] As in other chapters, all references to the GATT that do not specify a year are to GATT 1994 (which includes GATT 1947)—except that in Sections 8.2.2.3 through 8.3.2 of this chapter, references to the GATT that do not specify a year are to GATT 1947.

[2] Other WTO instruments include the about 60 agreements, annexes, decisions, and understandings that were adopted during the Uruguay Round, which is discussed in Section 8.4.3.2.

[3] Functional mechanisms are discussed in Chapter 7, Section 7.4.3.

The RCEP Agreement

Article 1.1 of the "Regional Comprehensive Economic Partnership Agreement,"[4] which came into effect on January 1, 2022, begins with the phrase: "The Parties, consistent with Article XXIV of GATT 1994, ..." The RCEP Agreement then references or cites the GATT, other WTO instruments, or WTO functional mechanisms (including WTO committees and the WTO DSB) another 86 times.

The predominance of the GATT and other WTO instruments, and the WTO mechanism, can be attributed to multiple factors, which include:

- Geographical scope: The areas of interest, application, and influence of the GATT instrument, other WTO instruments, and the WTO mechanism are global.[5]
- Participation: The parties to the GATT and other WTO instruments, and the WTO's members, include more than 80 percent of the world's nation-states (or 95 percent if WTO observers are included) and account for about 98 percent of international trade.
- Duration: The length of time the GATT instrument and other WTO instruments have been in effect, and that the de facto GATT organization and the WTO organization have been in operation.
- Mutual benefit: The primary operational provisions contained in the GATT instrument were designed as a plus-sum game.[6]
- Performance: The extraordinary effectiveness and success of the primary operational provisions contained in the GATT instrument.[7]

---

[4] The RCEP Agreement is discussed in Chapter 7, Section 7.3.2.1.
[5] Global instruments and mechanisms are discussed in Chapter 7, Section 7.2.2.
[6] Plus-sum games are discussed in Section 8.3.2; zero-sum games and minus-sum games are discussed in Sections 8.2.1.1 and 8.2.1.2.
[7] The extraordinary effectiveness and success of the GATT's primary operational provisions is discussed in Section 8.4.4.

8.2   The Origins of the GATT

For the reasons discussed in the previous section, it is impossible to fully understand the conduct of international trade and FDI unless we understand the primary operating provisions contained in the GATT. To understand these provisions, we must have some understanding of the origins and purposes of the instrument.

8.2.1   International Trade and the Great Depression

The factors that led to the creation of the GATT can be found in the international trade conditions that were present during the Great Depression, and that developed during the new political, security, and economic order that was created following the end of the Second World War (WWII).

The start of the Great Depression is generally attributed to structural weaknesses in the US economy, which resulted in the stock market crash of 1929. The severity and duration of the Great Depression are generally attributed to the escalation in the use of protectionist tariffs in the conduct of international trade,[8] which began in the United States with the adoption of the Tariff Act of 1930 (the Smoot–Hawley Tariff), which increased tariff barriers on more than 20,000 categories of products entering the US. The implementation of the Smoot–Hawley Tariff had two immediate effects. First, it reduced the value of imports entering the US by almost 50 percent. Second, it prompted Canada, the UK, and other countries to apply retaliatory tariffs to US products, which caused US exports to decline by more than 50 percent.[9]

8.2.1.1   Trade as a Zero-Sum Game

Over the next decade, the increased use of protectionist tariffs and retaliatory tariffs became a global phenomenon, because the governments of most nation-states saw the conduct of international trade as a zero-sum game—which is a win–lose situation, where the sum of the gains and the

---

[8] Protectionist tariffs are discussed in Chapter 2, Section 2.2.1.
[9] Irwin. "Peddling Protectionism: Smoot-Hawley and the Great Depression."

losses is zero. Zero-sum games are games of redistribution, where size of the pie does not change.[10]

8.2.1.2   The Minus-Sum Downward Spiral

The escalation of tariffs by nation-states in the 1930s, and the zero-sum mindset that dominated the international trade environment, led to the creation of a minus-sum game: a downward spiral that resulted in a more than 50 percent decline in international trade. A minus-sum game is a lose–lose situation, where all of the players lose. Minus-sum games are games of depletion, where the size of the pie is reduced.

The continued use of protectionist and retaliatory tariffs during the 1930s, further adversely affected the economies of individual countries and the global economy, and exacerbated and sustained the depression—which continued until the end of the Second World War.[11]

8.2.2   The New Political, Security, and Economic Order

The current concepts, principles, and structures that govern the conduct of international commerce are part of the new global political, security, and economic system that was established at the end of WWII.

8.2.2.1   The United Nations

The political and security factors of the post-WWII system are contained in the "Charter of the United Nations." This instrument was drafted and signed by representatives of 50 nation-states that met in San Francisco from April to June 1945, entered into force in October 1945, and created the United Nations organization.[12] The UN Charter also delineates the concepts, principles, and procedures that govern the policies and

---

[10] A zero-sum game is one of three game-theory alternatives. The other game-theory alternatives are minus-sum games, which are discussed in Section 8.2.1.2, and plus-sum games, which are discussed in Section 8.3.2.

[11] WWII began in 1937 in Asia and in 1939 in Europe, and ended in 1945.

[12] The first meeting of the United Nations organization was held in London in January 1946.

operations of the UN organization, the approximately 80 intergovernmental organizations that make up the UN System,[13] and the international political and security-related behaviors of UN member states.

8.2.2.2   The World Bank and the IMF

The economic elements of the post-WWII system include the International Bank for Reconstruction and Development (IBRD), which is commonly called the World Bank,[14] and the International Monetary Fund
(IMF). The treaties creating these two entities were finalized and signed
at the Bretton Woods Conference[15] in the United States in 1944. The
representatives of the 44 nation-states who attended the Bretton Woods
Conference also recommended the creation of a third mechanism that
would address international trade and other issues related to the conduct
of international commerce. The Bretton Woods Conference did not, however, initiate the creation of this third mechanism, because the conference
was attended primarily by ministers of finance, and not by ministers of
commerce and/or ministers of trade.

8.2.2.3   The Third Mechanism

The creation of the third mechanism followed two parallel tracks or
initiatives: (1) "The General Agreement on Tariffs and Trade,"[16] and
(2) the International Trade Organization (ITO).[17] The purpose of
the GATT initiative was to create a narrowly focused agreement that
would reduce tariffs and other barriers to trade. The purpose of the
ITO initiative was to create a treaty, the ITO Charter, that would govern all aspects of international trade—and would establish a global

---

[13] UN System, structure, and organization.

[14] The original purpose of the IBRD was to provide funding for the reconstruction of European countries after WWII. Its current purpose is the eradication of
poverty, by making loans to developing countries.

[15] The official name of the Bretton Woods Conference is the United Nations
Monetary and Financial Conference.

[16] In Sections 8.2.2.3 through 8.3.2 of this chapter, references to the GATT that
do not specify a year are to GATT 1947.

[17] The ITO initiative is discussed in Section 8.2.4.

organizational mechanism. Work on these two initiatives was interrelated and proceeded in parallel. The nation-states that participated in the GATT initiative also participated in the ITO initiative, and it was intended that the text of the GATT instrument would be included as a chapter of the ITO Charter.[18]

8.2.3   The GATT Initiative

The GATT initiative was characterized by a sense of urgency. The Second World War had caused huge loss of life, the destruction of property, and the dislocation and dysfunction of the global economy—and many world leaders believed that the extremely high tariffs that had been created during the 1930s threatened the recovery of the global economy.

In December 1945, at the invitation of the US government, representatives from 15 nation-states began talks related to the creation of a binding agreement for reducing tariffs. In October 1947, in Geneva, the participants in this initiative (which by then had increased to 23 nation-states) finalized work on the GATT instrument—which included tariff reductions on about 45,000 product categories[19] that were estimated to affect about 20 percent of world trade, and included a set of trade-related concepts, principles, and functional mechanisms.

8.2.3.1   The Implementation of the GATT Instrument

The term *agreement* was used in the title of the GATT to expedite its implementation. If the GATT instrument had been called a *treaty*, it would have been subject to ratification by the governments of the contracting parties, and to the possibility of protracted time delays that can accompany ratification processes.[20] As an agreement, the GATT instrument needed only definitive signature[21] by the required number of contracting parties—and could enter into force without being ratified. There was, however, a possibility that implementation of the

---

[18] The chapters of the ITO Charter are discussed in Section 8.2.4.1.

[19] Product categories are discussed in Chapter 2, Section 2.3.

[20] Ratification is discussed in Chapter 7, Section 7.3.2.1.

[21] Definitive signature is discussed in Chapter 7, Section 7.3.2.4.

GATT instrument could be delayed, because its acceptance requirements included an entry-into-force threshold.[22] This threshold, which was contained in Article XXVI, Acceptance, Entry into Force and Registration, required that the instrument be accepted by governments that "account for 85 per centum of the total external trade" of the countries participating in the process.

8.2.3.2   The Protocol of Provisional Application

To expedite implementation and avoid delays due to the 85 percent acceptance requirement, eight of the GATT contracting parties[23] signed a "Protocol of Provisional Application of the General Agreement on Tariffs and Trade" (PPA) on October 30, 1947, which caused Parts I, II, and III of the GATT—which included all of its primary operational provisions[24]—"to apply provisionally on and after January 1, 1948." The PPA was "provisional" because it was intended as a temporary measure to achieve immediate implementation of the primary operational provisions contained in the GATT—while waiting for the 85 percent acceptance requirement to be achieved and/or for the ITO Charter to enter into force.

The PPA was later signed by the other GATT initiative participants, and became the acceptance procedure used by all subsequent GATT contracting parties. In practice, the PPA replaced Article XXVI as the GATT's acceptance procedure.

8.2.4   The ITO Initiative

Whereas the GATT initiative was characterized by a sense of urgency, the ITO initiative was characterized by its scope: it was intended to cover all aspects of international trade. In February 1946, in response to proposals by the US and the UK, the United Nations Economic and Social

---

[22] Entry-into-force thresholds are discussed in Chapter 7, Section 7.3.2.2.

[23] The initial signatories to the PPA were Australia, Belgium, Canada, France, Luxemburg, the Netherlands, the UK, and the US.

[24] The GATT's primary operational provisions are discussed in Section 8.4.

Committee (UNESC) created a subcommittee to do preparatory work on the drafting of a charter for an International Trade Organization.

8.2.4.1   The ITO Charter

The meetings of the ITO subcommittee were held in London in 1946 and 1947. The drafting of the instrument was completed between November 1947 and March 1948, at the United Nations Conference on Trade and Employment in Havana. The ITO Charter was signed by 53 nation-states, in Lake Success, New York, in April, 1948. Chapter IV of the charter, Commercial Policy, included all of the operative articles from the GATT instrument. Chapter VII of the charter provided for the establishment of the ITO—and detailed the rules and procedures that would govern the structure, systems, and operations of the organization.

8.2.4.2   ITO Ratification

Article 103 of the ITO charter required that it be ratified before entering into force. Because the United States had led the ITO initiative, all other signatories chose to wait until the ITO Charter had been ratified by the US government before submitting it to their own governments for ratification. In April 1949, the president of the United States presented the ITO Charter to the US Congress for ratification, but it was never voted on by either house of the US Congress—and was not ratified by the United States.

Because the ITO Charter was not ratified by the United States, it was not ratified by any other signatory. Because it was not ratified by any signatory, the ITO Charter never entered into force, and the International Trade Organization was never created.

8.3   The GATT Instrument and Mechanism

As a result of the signing of the PPA, the primary operational provisions of the GATT entered into effect in January 1948, three months before the signing of the ITO Charter. Because the ITO Charter was not ratified by any signatory, and never entered into force, the International Trade Organization was never created—which meant there was no functional or organizational mechanism to provide logistical support for the implementation the GATT instrument.

8.3.1   GATT Operational Issues

The absence of a GATT functional or organizational mechanism[25] was solved in September 1948, by having the Interim Commission for the International Trade Organization (ICITO)—which had been established in March 1948 by the United Nations Economic and Social Council in Geneva to serve as the secretariat of the ITO—"provide secretariat services to the contracting parties of the GATT 1947."[26] Through this ad hoc arrangement, the ICITO became the de facto secretariat of the GATT, and continued unchanged in that capacity until December 31, 1994, after which the "assets, liabilities, records, staff, and functions of the ICITO and the GATT"[27] were transferred to the WTO Secretariat, which came into effect on January 1, 1995.

Because the ITO was not created, and because the GATT instrument did not provide for an organization, the signatories to the GATT instrument could not be called members—so were referred to as contracting parties. From January 1, 1948, until December 31, 1994, the GATT 1947 instrument (as amended and supplemented by a large number of related instruments) and the de facto GATT secretariat facilitated trade among the GATT contracting parties, which, by the end of 1994 included 125 nation-states and three separate customs territories.[28]

---

[25] Organizational and functional mechanisms are discussed in Chapter 7, Sections 7.4.2 and 7.4.3.

[26] ICTO/1/42. May 12, 1998. "Summary Record of the Meeting of the Executive Committee."

[27] ICTO/1/42. May 12, 1998. "Agreement on the Transfer of Assets, Liabilities, Records, Staff and Functions From the ICITO and the GATT to the WTO (WT/L/36)."

[28] The terms *nation-state* and *separate customs territory* are discussed in Chapter 7, Sections 7.1.1 and 7.1.3.

8.3.2   Reciprocal and Mutually Advantageous Arrangements

To reverse the effects of the escalation in tariff barriers by countries during the 1930s, which had resulted in a minus-sum downward spiral in international trade, the operative provisions contained in the GATT instrument were based on a plus-sum belief in mutual benefit—where all of the players win; and the size of the pie is increased.[29] The preamble to the GATT says that the relations between the contracting parties "should be conducted with a view to raising standards of living, ensuring full employment and a large and steadily growing volume of real income and effective demand, developing the full use of the resources of the world, and expanding the production and exchange of goods," and that the means for achieving these objectives would be "by entering into reciprocal and mutually advantageous arrangements" for "the substantial reduction of tariffs and other barriers to trade" and "the elimination of discriminatory treatment in international commerce."

8.4   The Primary Operational Provisions

The GATT instrument includes three primary operational provisions: (1) most-favored-nation (MFN), (2) national treatment, and (3) multilateral trade negotiations. The MFN and multilateral trade negotiations provisions are functional mechanisms[30] for reducing tariffs. The national treatment provision is a functional mechanism for eliminating discriminatory treatment against imported products.[31]

---

[29] A plus-sum game is one of three game-theory alternatives. The other game-theory alternatives are zero-sum games and minus-sum games, which are discussed in Sections 8.2.1.1 and 8.2.1.2.

[30] Functional mechanisms are discussed in Chapter 7, Section 7.4.3.

[31] Because GATT 1994 includes GATT 1947, these functional mechanisms are included in GATT 1994. The inclusion of GATT 1947 in GATT 1994 is discussed in Section 8.4.3.2.

8.4.1   Most-Favored-Nation

The "General Most-Favored-Nation Treatment" provision, which is contained in Article I of the GATT, is a continuous functional mechanism for reducing tariffs.

8.4.1.1   The MFN Concept

In the conduct of international trade, when a country lowers or removes tariff barriers, NTBs, or other barriers to trade with another country, this has the effect of providing that country with a competitive trade advantage. The lowering or removing of trade barriers with another country is, therefore, referred to as providing that country with a trade advantage or preference.[32]

The country that applies the lowest level of trade barriers to the importation of products from another country is called that country's *most-favored nation*. The concept that is now referred to as most-favored-nation or MFN, provides that—when the MFN provision is included in a trade agreement—the countries that are party to the agreement must offer or grant to the other party or parties to the agreement the same low level of trade barriers as they have granted their most-favored nation.

The use of this concept can be seen in trade agreements between European countries, dating from the 15th century.[33] In most cases, the concept was used as a parity maintaining mechanism. The purpose of the provision was to assure parties to trade agreements that the terms they had negotiated and agreed to would not be eclipsed by the terms that one of the parties could subsequently grant to one or more other countries. The MFN parity maintaining mechanism is progressive, because, instead of the parties promising not to grant more favorable terms to other countries, the parties are promising that if they grant more favorable terms to another country—they will offer

---

[32] Preferences are discussed in Chapter 7, Sections 7.1.6.

[33] *The Most-Favored-Nation Provision, Executive Branch Study No. 9*, p. 1.

or grant these same more favorable terms (that they have granted to their most-favored nation) to the other party or parties to the present agreement.

8.4.1.2   Conditional and Unconditional Forms

The MFN concept takes two forms: conditional and unconditional. The distinction between the two forms rests on the presence or absence of a reciprocity requirement.

1. The conditional form of MFN requires that any preference that has been granted to the most-favored nation must be offered to the other party or parties to the agreement—but that the granting of the preference is subject to the offering party receiving a reciprocal advantage.
2. The unconditional form requires that the preference must be granted to the other party or parties to the agreement—without the granting party receiving any reciprocal advantage.

8.4.1.3   The Origins of the Term

The term *most-favored-nation* is from the noun phrase "Nations most favored," from Article 3 of the "Treaty of Amity and Commerce Between the American states and France of 1778." When the treaty was being negotiated, the 13 American colonies were engaged in their war of independence with England. Before the war (consistent with traditional colony-metropole trade practices), the tariffs on imports from England into the commerce of the American colonies were significantly lower than the tariffs on imports from France and other countries.

During the treaty negotiations, instead of negotiating specific tariff rates, the foreign minister of France, Charles de Vergennes (who had been a career foreign service officer, had held several foreign diplomatic appointments, and had extensive experience with trade and defense agreements) provided the Commissioners from the American colonies[34] with the language that was included verbatim in Article 3 of the treaty.[35] This language says that, in the United States [sic], the subjects of the king of France "shall pay ... no other or greater Duties or Imposts ... by what Name soever called, than those which the *Nations most favored* [emphasis added] are or shall be obliged to pay; and they shall enjoy all the Rights, Liberties, Privileges, Immunities and Exemptions in Trade, Navigation and Commerce ... which the said Nations do or shall enjoy."

The term came into regular usage in the second half of the 19th century, beginning with the unconditional most-favored-nation clause contained in the 1860 "Cobden–Chevalier Treaty," between Great Britain and France, which was initiated by the British but drafted by the French. Over the next decade the term was used in seven trade treaties that were entered into by Great Britain, which was at the time the world's leading trading nation.[36]

8.4.1.4   Conditional and Unconditional Usage

Before 1778, the usage of the MFN concept by European countries was, in most cases, unconditional. But the MFN provision contained in the "Treaty of Amity and Commerce of 1778" was conditional. Article 2 of this treaty says that neither party shall "grant any particular Favor to other Nations in respect of Commerce or Navigation, which shall not immediately become common to the other Party, who shall enjoy the same Favor, freely, if the Concession was freely made, or on allowing the same Compensation, if the Concession was Conditional." This language includes both unconditional and conditional elements, but because it includes references to compensation, it is seen as being conditional.

---

[34] The Commissioners from the Continental Congress to France were Benjamin Franklin, Arthur Lee, and Silas Deane.

[35] Davies. n.d. *International Business and US Foreign Policy*, p. 139.

[36] Beunderman. n.d. *A Century of International Trade Policy 1840—1940*, p. 7. *The Most-Favored-Nation Provision, Executive Branch Study No. 9*, p. 2 and 3.

Following the use of the unconditional most-favored-nation clause in the 1860 "Cobden–Chevalier Treaty," with some exceptions, most European countries continued their previous practice of using unconditional MFN provisions in their trade agreements, and Japan and countries in Central and South America used both forms.[37] During this period, the United States used conditional MFN provisions in its trade agreements, until the adoption of the Tariff Act of 1922, and the Trade Agreements Act of 1934—which authorized the US government to use unconditional MFN provisions. This change in US trade policy was fortuitous, because it brought the US into concert with the MFN usage practices of European countries—and in 1947 allowed the US government to agree to the provisions contained in the MFN clause in Article I of the GATT, which states that the granting of MFN advantages shall be unconditional.

8.4.1.5   The GATT MFN Clause

The operative language from Article I, paragraph 1, of the GATT, which is commonly referred to as the *most-favored-nation clause*, says that "with respect to customs duties .... any advantage, favor, privilege or immunity granted by any member to any product" from any country "shall be accorded immediately and unconditionally to the like product originating in or destined for the territories of all other members."

> Note concerning US terminology: Since the adoption of the Internal Revenue Restructuring and Reform Act of 1998,[38] United States law has referred to *most-favored-nation* as *normal trade relations*. But some US executive branch documents use the term *most-favored-nation*.

The language in the MFN clause refers specifically to trade in products, which was later seen as not covering trade in services. This led, during

---

[37] Ibid.

[38] Internal Revenue Restructuring and Reform Act of 1998, P.L. 105–206 § 5003, 112 Stat. 685 (1998).

the Uruguay Round of multilateral trade negotiations, to the adoption of "General Agreement on Trade in Services" (GATS).[39]

8.4.1.6   The GATT MFN Process

The tariff-reducing process contained in the GATT MFN clause is simple. To facilitate the export of their products, countries are continually negotiating tariff reductions with other countries. Because the MFN clause contained in the GATT is unconditional, the lower tariffs agreed to in trade negotiations between WTO members must, with some exceptions,[40] be granted to all WTO members.

> The US: Trucks
>
> The tariff on trucks entering the United States is 25 percent. If the US government were to reduce the tariff on trucks entering the US from Japan to 20 percent, then, for this category of product, Japan would be the US's most favored nation. Because the US is a member of the WTO, and because none of the exceptions discussed in Section 8.4.1.4 currently apply to Japan, the US would be required by the provisions contained in the MFN clause to reduce the tariff rate on trucks from all WTO members to 20 percent.

This process is also ingenious. The governments of countries are motivated by national self-interest to continuously negotiate and enter into trade agreements that reduce tariffs and other trade barriers with other countries—because they believe that the preferences contained in these agreements will facilitate exports by their nationals and, therefore, benefit their national economy. Although these actions are driven by national self-interest, they result in mutual benefit and produce bilateral plus-sum games.[41] By mandating that trade preferences contained in bilateral

---

[39] The Uruguay Round is discussed in Section 8.4.3.2. The GATS is discussed in Section 8.5.3.1.
[40] Exceptions to the MFN requirement are discussed in Section 8.4.1.4.
[41] Plus-sum games are discussed in Section 8.3.2.

trade agreements be extended unconditionally to all WTO members, the GATT MFN requirement reduces global tariff levels and reduces global barriers to trade—and converts the cumulation of multiple bilateral plus-sum games into a global multilateral plus-sum game.

8.4.1.7   Exceptions to the MFN Requirement

The GATT allows several exceptions to the MFN requirement. These exceptions include historical preferences that were in force at the signing of the GATT (Article I);[42] measures necessary to protect public morals, life, and health (Article XX); security exceptions (Article XXI); frontier traffic with adjacent countries (Article XXIV); and the Generalized System of Preferences for products from less-developed countries[43] (Article XXXVI). Also, the language contained in Article XXIV, paragraphs 5 to 8, of the GATT is seen as saying that the MFN requirement does not apply to the substantial elimination of "duties and other restrictive regulations of commerce"[44] between members of regional trade blocs. This exception is discussed in Chapter 9, Sections 9.3.2 and 9.5.3.

8.4.2   National Treatment

The "National Treatment on Internal Taxation and Regulation" provision, which is contained in Article III of the GATT, is a functional mechanism for eliminating "discriminatory treatment in international commerce." The "national treatment" provision was intended to facilitate trade by preventing discrimination against imported products after they have entered a country.

Article III, paragraph 2, which is often referred to as the "national treatment clause," says that: "the products of the territory of any Member imported into the territory of any other Member shall not be subject, directly or indirectly, to internal taxes or other internal charges of any

---

[42] Preferences are discussed in Chapter 7, Sections 7.1.6.

[43] The terms *developing countries* and *least developed countries* are discussed in Chapter 7, Sections 7.1.2.2 and 7.1.2.3.

[44] Article XXIV, paragraph 8(b) of the GATT.

kind in excess of those applied, directly or indirectly, to like domestic products" and that these products will "be accorded treatment no less favorable than that accorded to like products of national origin in respect of all laws, regulations and requirements affecting their internal sale, offering for sale, purchase, transportation, distribution or use."

The national treatment clause contained in the GATT refers to the treatment of products, and does not address the treatment of entities engaged in the conduct of international commerce. This distinction is important, because the "Agreement on Trade-Related Investment Measures" (TRIMs), which was one of the Uruguay Round agreements,[45] extended the application of the national treatment clause, and other provisions of Article III of the GATT, to cover investment—and the treatment of foreign-funded companies that are engaged in the conduct of FDI. This extension is discussed in Sections 8.5.3 and 8.5.3.2.

8.4.3   Multilateral Trade Negotiations

The "Tariff Negotiations" provision, which is contained in Article XXVIII of the GATT, is a periodic functional mechanism for reducing tariffs "and other charges on imports and exports." Article XXVIII (1) provides that "the contracting parties may therefore sponsor such negotiations from time to time." Article XXVIII (2)(b) provides that "the success of multilateral negotiations would depend on the participation of all contracting parties which conduct a substantial proportion of their external trade with one another."

The tariff negotiations provided for in Article XXVIII are commonly referred to as *multilateral trade negotiations*. Each set of periodic negotiations is called a *trade round* or simply as a *round*. Between 1949 and the end of 1994, the GATT contracting parties participated in and concluded seven rounds of multilateral trade negotiations. Each round was named after the city or country in which the GATT contracting parties were meeting when the round was initiated, or, in two cases, after a person.

---

[45] The Uruguay Round agreements are discussed in Section 8.4.3.2.

8.4.3.1   The Annecy to Tokyo Rounds

Each round has tended to focus on one or more issue areas. During the Annecy (1949), Torquay (1951), and Geneva (1955–1956) rounds, the contracting parties focused on further reducing tariffs on existing product categories and adding new categories. In subsequent rounds, the contracting parties continued to reduce tariffs, but also began addressing other issue areas that drove the evolution of the GATT 1947 instrument and the de facto GATT organization. The Dillon Round (1960–1962) addressed issues related to the creation of the European Economic Community (EEC); the Kennedy Round (1964–1967) addressed anti-dumping and rules relating to trade negotiations; and the Tokyo Round (1973–1979) developed rules and procedures relating to anti-dumping, licensing, non-tariff barriers, and the settlement of disputes—and resulted in the adoption of five plurilateral agreements.[46]

8.4.3.2   The Uruguay Round

The Uruguay Round (1986–1994) addressed tariffs on textiles and agriculture, non-tariff barriers, trade in services, intellectual property, and the settlement of disputes. The Uruguay Round resulted in the adoption of about 60 agreements, annexes, decisions, and understandings—which included the GATS, TRIPS,[47] and TRIMs;[48] the "Agreement on Rules of Origin";[49] the multilateral 1994 "Agreement on Technical Barriers to Trade" (TBT agreement), which had been adopted as a plurilateral agreement during the Tokyo Round;[50] and a new "General Agreement on Tariffs and Trade" (GATT 1994).

---

[46] Plurilateral agreements are discussed in Section 8.4.3.3.

[47] GATS and TRIPS are discussed in Sections 8.5.3 and 8.5.3.1.

[48] TRIMs is discussed in Sections 8.4.2, 8.5.3, and 8.5.3.2 of this chapter; and Chapter 9, Section 9.2.2.

[49] The Agreement on Rules of Origin is discussed in Chapter 2, Sections 2.4.2 and 2.4.3.

[50] Multilateral and plurilateral agreements are discussed in Section 8.4.3.3. The TBT agreement is discussed in Chapter 10, Section 10.2, and other sections of Chapter 10.

To differentiate the 1947 and 1994 GATT instruments, they are referred to as GATT 1947 and GATT 1994. GATT 1994 includes all of the provisions contained in GATT 1947, together with its amendments. References to the GATT that do not specify a year are to GATT 1994 and, therefore, to both instruments. Because of a provision contained in GATT 1994, Article 2(a),[51] when reading or citing from GATT 1947 as part of GATT 1994, it is necessary to change the term *contracting party* to *member*.

The participants in the Uruguay Round also drafted and adopted the "Agreement Establishing the WTO." Because this instrument was signed at the 1994 ministerial meeting in Marrakesh, it is commonly called the "Marrakesh Agreement" (MA). The implementation of the MA and its provisions are discussed in Section 8.5.

8.4.3.3   Multilateral and Plurilateral Agreements

In the fields of international relations and international commerce, the term *multilateral* refers to agreements, mechanisms, or other relationships that include participation by three or more nation-states.[52] The term is used three times in the GATT (in Article XXVIII and Annex I, Article XXVIII), and each of these usages is consistent with this meaning. During the Tokyo Round of multilateral trade negotiations (1973–1979),[53] however, the term *multilateral* was given an additional meaning—when select groups of GATT contracting parties entered into five agreements: the "Agreement on Trade in Civil Aircraft"; the "Agreement on Government Procurement"; the "International Dairy Agreement"; the "International Bovine Meat Agreement";[54] and the "Agreement on Technical Barriers to Trade."[55] The rationale for the limited participation in these agreements was that each of these agreements addressed a single category of

---

[51] GATT 1994, Article 2(a), says that "references to contracting party in the provisions of GATT 1994 shall be deemed to read Member."

[52] See Chapter 7, Section 7.2.2.

[53] See Section 8.4.3.1.

[54] These dairy and bovine meat agreements were terminated in 1997.

[55] This plurilateral Agreement on Technical Barriers to Trade, and the 1994 multilateral TBT agreement, are discussed in Chapter 10, Section 10.2.

products (or, in the case of governmental procurement, a single category of processes), that was of particular importance to a limited group of contracting parties.

The entering into these agreements by select groups of GATT contracting parties was an innovation, because until then all decisions by the contracting parties of the de facto GATT organization required *unanimous approval* or *consensus*,[56] which meant that all agreements between the GATT contracting parties required participation by all contracting parties. To distinguish the Tokyo Round agreements that included participation by all of the GATT contracting parties from the five agreements that included participation by a select group of contracting parties, the former were referred to as *multilateral* agreements; the latter were called *plurilateral* agreements. Following the coining of this new additional meaning for the term *multilateral*, and the addition of the term *plurilateral* during the Tokyo Round, these terms entered into the lexicons of the de facto GATT organization and of its successor organization, the WTO. For example, on the WTO website, the two categories in the WTO's Status of Legal Instruments are *Multilateral Agreements on Trade in Goods* and *Plurilateral Agreements on Trade in Goods*.[57]

8.4.4   The Extraordinary Success of the GATT

Based on its stated objectives, the success of the GATT 1947 instrument and its implementation by the de facto GATT organization from January 1, 1948, until December 31, 1994, was extraordinary. By the end of 1994, tariffs, non-tariff barriers, other barriers to trade, and discriminatory treatment in international trade were a fraction of the levels they had been in 1947. These reductions in trade barriers were reflected in increases in the volume of world trade. "World trade in 1948 amounted to $54 billion; by 1958, it had reached $95 billion, and by 1970, $280 billion. United States exports expanded from $13 billion in 1948 to $43 billion in 1970."[58] This extraordinary success was due to the effectiveness of the

---

[56] Unanimous approval and consensus are discussed in Section 8.5.1.2

[57] WTO's Status of Legal Instruments.

[58] *The Most-Favored-Nation Provision, Executive Branch Study No. 9*, p. 4.

three primary operational provisions contained in the GATT instrument, and to the implementation and administration of these provisions by the de facto GATT organization.

8.5   The Establishment of the WTO

From January 1, 1948, until December 31, 1994, GATT 1947 and related instruments were implemented and administered by the de facto GATT organization. On January 1, 1995, the "Agreement Establishing the WTO" (the "Marrakesh Agreement"), GATT 1994, and about 60 other instruments concluded under the Uruguay Round entered into force.

Article 1 of the "Marrakesh Agreement" is one line, which says: "The World Trade Organization (hereinafter referred to as the WTO) is hereby established." The organizational provisions contained in the MA replaced the de facto GATT organization. The principal differences between the de facto GATT organization and the WTO relate to structure, membership, and scope.

8.5.1   Structure

The "Marrakesh Agreement" details the terms and conditions governing the establishment of the WTO; and the terms and conditions covering its structure, administration, and operations.

8.5.1.1   The Secretariat, Bodies, and Hierarchy

Article VI of the MA says the WTO shall have a "Secretariat," "headed by a Director-General." On January 1, 1995, the de facto GATT Secretariat, located in Geneva, became the WTO Secretariat; the Director-General of the GATT became the Director-General of the WTO.

Article XVI of the MA says the "WTO shall be guided by the decisions, procedures and customary practices followed by the contracting parties to GATT 1947 and the bodies established in the framework of GATT 1947." Article IV of the MA defines a hierarchy of deliberative and decision-making bodies. The highest deliberative and decision making body of the WTO is the Ministerial Conference, "which shall meet at least once every two years" and "shall carry out the functions of the WTO and take actions necessary to this effect."

All members of the WTO are members of the Ministerial Conference. Participation in the Ministerial Conference is by a minister (or secretary) of commerce, trade, finance, foreign affairs, agriculture, or other ministerial-level representative from each WTO member. Article VI says the Ministerial Conference appoints the Director-General of the WTO, and defines "the powers, duties, conditions of service, and term of office of the Director-General." The second-level deliberative and decision-making bodies, which operate continuously, are the General Council, the Dispute Settlement Body, and the Trade Policy Review Body. All members of the WTO are members of these second-level bodies, which report to the Ministerial Conference. The third-level bodies include the Council for Trade in Goods (Goods Council), the Council for Trade in Services (Services Council), the Council for Trade-Related Aspects of Intellectual Property Rights (TRIPS Council), and six committees that address specific areas. The fourth level includes numerous committees that report to the second- or third-level bodies or councils.

8.5.1.2   Decision-Making

Article XXV (4) of GATT 1947 says that, with some exceptions, decisions "shall be taken by a majority of the votes cast"—and neither the terms *unanimous approval* nor *consensus* appear in GATT 1947. In practice, however, decisions by the contracting parties of the de facto GATT organization were adopted by consensus. Article IX of the MA says the "WTO shall continue the practice of decision-making by consensus followed under GATT 1947." The "majority of the votes cast" language contained Article XXV (4) of GATT 1947 was not amended by the MA or by GATT 1994, but the language contained in Article IX of the MA codifies the continuation of the practice of decision-making by consensus.

Article IX of the MA also says if the members are unable to reach a consensus, in most cases "the matter at issue shall be decided by voting" and "decisions of the Ministerial Conference and the General Council shall be taken by a majority of the votes cast." The exceptions to the simple majority requirement are: (1) membership decisions, which require a two-thirds majority; (2) the waiver of a member's obligation, which requires a three-fourths majority; and (3) amendments to the MA and other WTO instruments, some of which can require a two-thirds majority, a three-fourths majority, or, in some cases, unanimous approval.

8.5.2   *Membership*

Article XI of the "Marrakesh Agreement" provides for GATT 1947 contracting parties to become original members of the WTO by signing and ratifying the instruments concluded under the Uruguay Round. Article XII of the MA provides for the accession of other members.

8.5.2.1   Separate Customs Territories

The members of many intergovernmental organizations, such as the UN, are referred to as *member states*. The members of the WTO, however, are called *members*. This is because Article XII of the MA provides that membership in the WTO is open to nation-states—and to any "separate customs territory possessing full autonomy in the conduct of its external commercial relations."[59] The membership of the WTO includes four SCTs. Three of these, the European Union, Hong Kong,[60] and Macao, had been contracting parties of the GATT, and became WTO members in 1995. Taiwan became a WTO member in 2002.[61]

8.5.2.2   Members and Observers

The WTO has 164 members and 25 observers. Article XII of the MA, which allows for separate customs territories to be members, also allows for them to be observers. All WTO observers, with the exception of the

---

[59] The definition and use of the term *separate customs territory* in Article XII of the MA were borrowed from Article XXXIII of GATT 1947. The term *separate customs territory* is discussed in Chapter 7, Section 7.1.3.

[60] Hong Kong is listed by the WTO as Hong Kong, China.

[61] Taiwan joined under the name "Separate Customs Territory of Taiwan, Penghu, Kinmen, and Matsu (Chinese Taipei)," and is listed by the WTO as Chinese Taipei.

Holy See (the Vatican), must begin membership negotiations within five years after becoming an observer. The accession of new WTO members, and the terms contained in their accession agreements, require approval by the Ministerial Conference. Although Article XII of the MA says these approvals require a two-thirds majority vote, to date all accession decisions have been by consensus.

8.5.3   Expanded Scope and Functions

Articles II and III of the "Marrakesh Agreement" define the scope and functions of the WTO, which include all of the functions that were formerly performed by the de facto GATT organization—together with some additional functions. The most significant of these new functions are contained in three of the Uruguay Round instruments: the "General Agreement on Trade in Services" (GATS), the "Agreement on Trade-Related Aspects of Intellectual Property Rights" (TRIPS), and the "Agreement on Trade-Related Investment Measures" (TRIMs).

8.5.3.1   Trade in Services and Intellectual Property

The scope of the GATT 1947 instrument and the de facto GATT organization was limited to trade in products (which is also referred to as trade in goods). The scope of the WTO includes two additional areas of trade: (1) trade in services and (2) trade in intellectual property. These new trade areas are covered by provisions contained in the MA, GATS, and TRIPS agreements. Because of the expansion and importance of trade in services and intellectual property that had occurred since the GATT 1947 instrument entered into effect on January 1, 1948, this expansion was seen as necessary. Also, this expansion appeared innocuous. But the implementation of the intellectual property rights provisions contained in the TRIPs agreement (which has included treating medicines as consumer products, which has limited the ability of developing countries and least developed countries[62] to access desperately needed medicines at reasonable prices) exacerbated the North–South divisions during the

---

[62] The terms *developing countries* and *least developed countries* are discussed in Chapter 7, Sections 7.1.2.2 and 7.1.2.3.

Doha Round of multilateral trade negotiations, led to the adoption of the "Declaration on the TRIPS Agreement and Public Health," and has led to what is referred to as the *TRIPS plus enforcement trend* (or *TRIPS plus*).

8.5.3.2   The Addition of Investment

The most radical difference between the scope of the de facto GATT organization and the scope of the WTO, is that the WTO and its instruments cover both trade and investment. The national treatment clause of the GATT[63] refers solely to trade in products—and does not refer to investment, or to the treatment of foreign-funded companies that are engaged in the conduct of FDI. The "Agreement on Trade-Related Investment Measures" (TRIMs) extended the application of the national treatment clause, and other provisions of Article III of the GATT, to cover investment—and the foreign-funded companies that are engaged in the conduct of FDI.

This change was radical because, since its inception, the GATT instrument and the de facto GATT organization had focused solely on the trade half of the trade–investment dichotomy. Unlike the addition of services and intellectual property, which appeared necessary and innocuous, the expansion of the scope of the national treatment clause to include investment, and the treatment of foreign-funded companies that are engaged in the conduct of FDI, were two of the four contentious issues that came to dominate the first WTO Ministerial Conference, which was held in Singapore, in December 1996.[64] As with the implementation of the provisions contained in the TRIPs agreement, the TRIMS investment provisions exacerbated the North–South divisions that contributed to the failure of the Doha Round of multilateral trade negotiations. Representatives from some developing countries argued against the investment and national treatment Singapore Issues, on the grounds that, by definition, the WTO's mandate is limited to trade— and that investment issues should be handled by other intergovernmental

---

[63] See Section 8.4.2.

[64] The investment and national treatment Singapore Issues are discussed in Chapter 9, Section 9.2.2.

mechanisms, such as UNCTAD.[65] Also, at and following the Singapore conference, many representatives from developing countries voiced their strong concern that the areas covered by the investment and national treatment Singapore Issues were not mutually beneficial: that they were designed to benefit developed countries and their nationals who are engaged in the practice of international trade and/or FDI—at the expense of developing countries.

8.6   WTO Operational Issues

A supplemental reading on WTO operational issues is available from the book's web page. This reading covers critical WTO developments since the 1996 Singapore Ministerial Conference—which include the Singapore Issues, the emergence of the North–South zero-sum game, the adjournment of Cancún Ministerial Conference, the Doha Round Issues, and the failure of the Doha Round. The reading also discusses the effects of the operational issues, and the causal relationship between the operational issues and the increased use of plurilateral agreements and preferential trade agreements.

---

[65] UNCTAD is discussed in Chapter 7, Section 7.1.2.3.

CHAPTER 9

Regional and Bilateral Instruments and Mechanisms

Contents

9.1   Regional Integration

When nation-states from the same geographical region cooperate for the purpose of achieving economic, political, social, cultural, security-related, and/or other mutually beneficial goals—this is referred to as regional integration.

9.1.1   Regional Integration Agreements

The instruments that nation-states negotiate, enter into, implement, and administer to effect regional integration are called regional integration agreements (RIAs). The creation of RIAs is driven by their participants' geographical proximity. In some cases, RIAs address a wide range of political, economic, and/or security-related areas—but all RIAs focus on operational issues that are of specific importance to their geographical region or sub-region.

ASEAN

In 1967, Indonesia, Malaysia, Philippines, Singapore, and Thailand signed an instrument called "The ASEAN Declaration," which created the Association of Southeast Asian Nations. The preamble to the declaration states that ASEAN was being created to "accelerate the economic growth, social progress, and cultural development in the region" and to "promote regional peace and stability."

The GCC

In 1981, Bahrain, Kuwait, Oman, Qatar, Saudi Arabia, and the United Arab Emirates created the Cooperation Council for the Arab States of the Gulf, which is commonly called the Gulf Cooperation Council (GCC), "to effect coordination, integration and inter-connection between Member States in all fields in order to achieve unity between them."[1]

Other RIAs include: the African Union (AU); the Andean Community (Pacto Andino); the Commonwealth of Independent States (CIS); the Gulf Cooperation Council (GCC); the North Atlantic Treaty Organization (NATO); the Shanghai Cooperation Organization (SCO); the South Asian Association for Regional Cooperation (SAARC); and the West African Economic and Monetary Union (WAEMU).

The initialism RIA can refer to: (1) a regional integration agreement; or (2) a regional integration area. The term *regional integration area* can mean: (1) the geographical area covered by the countries that are participants in a regional integration agreement, and/or (2) the functional or organizational mechanism that is used to implement and administer a regional integration agreement.

9.1.2   Levels of Integration

The term *level of integration* refers to the degree to which an RIA is integrated—and the extent to which its member states have surrendered parts of their sovereignty.[2] When referring to an RIA's level of integration, the terms *limited integration* and *deep integration* define the ends of a continuum.

ASEAN

When ASEAN was created, it was at the limited-integration end of the continuum: its founding members created an association that would facilitate cooperation, but would not require them to give up any parts of their sovereignty. Since then, ASEAN

---

[1] GCC Charter, Article 4.
[2] The partial surrender of sovereignty is discussed in Chapter 7, Section 7.1.5.3.

has created a Secretariat, has added five additional members,[3] has established the ASEAN Free Trade Area,[4] and has become a more deeply integrated RIA.

EU

The RIA with the deepest level of integration is the European Union. The origins and evolution of the EU are discussed in Section 9.2.1.2.

9.2   Regional Trade Blocks

If the purpose of a regional integration instrument is to effect economic integration and create mutual economic benefit by reducing or eliminating barriers to trade and FDI—it is called a regional trade agreement (RTA), or a regional preferential trade agreement (regional PTA).[5]

The entity created by an RTA/regional PTA is called a *regional trade block* or *regional trading block* (RTB).[6] The term RTB is used when referring to: (1) the group of countries that are parties to a regional PTA, and (2) the mechanism that is used to implement and administer the provisions contained in an RTA/regional PTA. According to the OECD,[7] more than half of the world's trade occurs within RTBs.

RTBs include: the African Continental Free Trade Area (AfCFTA); the ASEAN Free Trade Area (ASEAN FTA); the Caribbean Community and Common Market (CARICOM); the Central American Common Market (CACM); the China–ASEAN Free Trade Area (ACFTA); the Common Market for Eastern and Southern Africa; the Comprehensive and Progressive Agreement for Trans-Pacific Partnership (CPTPP); the Digital Economy Partnership Agreement (DEPA); the Economic Community of West African States (ECOWAS); the Economic and

---

[3] The ASEAN member states are: Brunei, Cambodia, Indonesia, Laos, Malaysia, Myanmar, Philippines, Singapore, Thailand, and Vietnam.

[4] The ASEAN FTA is discussed in Section 9.3.3.

[5] PTAs are discussed in Chapter 7, Section 7.1.6.

[6] Although the term *regional trade bloc* refers specifically to trade, most RTBs also facilitate FDI between their member states.

[7] OECD Regional Trade Agreements.

Monetary Community of Central Africa; the Eurasian Economic Union (EAEU); the European Free Trade Area (EFTA); the European Union (EU); the Gulf Cooperation Council (GCC); the Indian Ocean Commission; the Latin America and Andean Pact (Pacto Andino); the Latin American Integration Association (LAIA); the Regional Comprehensive Economic Partnership (RCEP); the South Asian Association for Regional Cooperation; the Southern African Development Community (SADC); the Southern Cone Common Market (MERCOSUR); the Sub-Saharan Africa Cross-Border Initiative; the United States, Mexico, Canada Agreement (USMCA); and the West African Economic and Monetary Union.

9.2.1   RTB Functions

RTBs facilitate regional economic integration, and create mutual economic benefit for their members, by:

- Reducing or eliminating tariff, non-tariff barriers, and other barriers to trade;
- Reducing entry and post-entry barriers to FDI;
- Providing the regulatory and operational parameters that govern or influence the conduct of trade and FDI between their members; and
- Providing mechanisms for the harmonization of laws that affect the conduct of regional commerce, and for the settlement of regional commercial disputes.[8]

9.2.1.1   NAFTA–USMCA

In 1993, Canada, Mexico, and the United States entered into the "North American Free Trade Agreement,"[9] which, on January 1, 1994, created an RTB called the North American Free Trade Area (NAFTA). Article 102

---

[8] The harmonization of laws is discussed in Chapter 11. The settlement of disputes is discussed in Chapter 12.

[9] This agreement superseded the 1987 Canada–US Free Trade Agreement.

of the NAFTA instrument listed six objectives: to eliminate barriers to trade; promote fair competition; increase investment opportunities; protect intellectual property rights; create procedures for the implementation and administration of the agreement and for the resolution of disputes; and to establish a framework for further cooperation.

In 2017, the members of NAFTA began negotiations to revise the agreement. The resulting revisions changed some of the product-related provisions—and especially those relating to automotive, textile, and agriculture products; changed some of the rules of origin procedures; changed product content requirements and limits; increased the life of intellectual property rights; added provisions relating to the storage of trade-related digital information; included provisions that have not traditionally been included in trade agreements—which cover human rights protections, environmental protections, and minimum wage levels for some employees;[10] and changed the name of the instrument to the "United States, Mexico, Canada Agreement" (USMCA). The revised and renamed agreement came into effect on July 1, 2020.

9.2.1.2   The European Union

The European Union is near the deep-integration end of the continuum. The origins of this integration began in 1951, when six European countries,[11] led by France, signed "The Europe Declaration"[12] (which stated the signatories' determination to create a "supranational institution" and to lay the "foundation of an organized Europe") and entered into the "Treaty of Paris," which created the European Coal and Steel Community (ESEC).[13] The end purpose of the ECSC, which eliminated trade barriers on coal and steel, was not primarily economic—but was

---

[10] Some of these provisions had previously been contained in side agreements. The minimum wage provision contained in the USMCA is discussed in Chapter 10, Section 10.5.2.

[11] Belgium, France, West Germany, Italy, Luxembourg, and the Netherlands.

[12] The "Europe Declaration" is also referred to as the "Charter of the Community," and as the "Schuman Declaration," after French foreign minister Robert Schuman.

[13] The official name of the "Treaty of Paris" is the "Treaty Establishing the European Coal and Steel Community" (1951).

to facilitate and enhance socio-political, diplomatic, and economic integration and stability, and thereby to mitigate the perceived threat of a resurgent Germany.[14]

In 1957, these same six countries entered into the "Treaty of Rome,"[15] which created the European Economic Community (EEC); stated the intention of the parties to eliminate trade barriers between the member states, to establish common trade barriers and policies with third countries, and to abolish "obstacles to the free movement of persons, services, and capital" between the member states;[16] and created a secretariat, called the European Commission. In 1986, the Single European Act gave effect to some of these provisions, and established the EEC as a customs union.[17] In 1992, the EEC members entered into the "Maastricht Treaty,"[18] which furthered their regional integration by, inter alia, creating the European Union (EU); changing the name of the EEC to the European Community, and including it as a founding element of the EU; establishing a directly elected European Parliament; providing for the future establishment of a monetary union; and by giving full effect to many of the provisions contained in the "Treaty of Rome."

The EU now includes shared political, juridical, and banking institutions; shared foreign policy and military policy; shared legal systems and laws, regulations, and product standards; a monetary union;[19] the right of its citizens to live and work in any member country; and includes 27 members.[20] The EU's organizational elements include a political body (the European Council), a legislative body (the European Parliament), and an executive body (the European Commission).

---

[14] See Ireland. n.d. "Creating the Entangling Alliance."

[15] The official name of the "Treaty of Rome" is the "Treaty Establishing the European Economic Community." This treaty entered into force in 1958.

[16] Part One—Principles, Article 3, paragraphs (a), (b), and (c), of the "Treaty Establishing the European Economic Community."

[17] Customs unions are discussed in Section 9.4.

[18] The official name of the "Maastricht Treaty" is the "Treaty on European Union." The treaty entered into force in 1993.

[19] Not all EU member countries are members of the European Monetary Union.

[20] The EU member states are: Austria, Belgium, Bulgaria, Croatia, Cyprus, the Czech Republic, Denmark, Estonia, Finland, France, Germany, Greece, Hungary, Ireland, Italy, Latvia, Lithuania, Luxembourg, Malta, Netherlands, Poland, Portugal, Romania, Slovakia, Slovenia, Spain, and Sweden.

9.2.1.3   The TPSEP/TPP/CPTPP

In 2001, New Zealand and Singapore entered into the "Agreement between New Zealand and Singapore on a Closer Economic Partnership," which in 2006 became the "Trans-Pacific Strategic Economic Partnership Agreement" (TPSEP), which included Brunei, Chile, New Zealand, and Singapore. This agreement was called a comprehensive trade agreement, because, in addition to addressing tariffs, NTBs and other barriers to trade in products, it addressed trade in services, rules of origin, dispute settlement, intellectual property, government procurement, and competition. In February 2016, the four TPSEP members, plus Australia, Canada, Japan, Malaysia, Mexico, Peru, Vietnam, and the United States signed the "Trans-Pacific Partnership Agreement" (TPP). In February 2017, the United States withdrew from the agreement. The withdrawal by the US meant that the TPP agreement could not enter into force, even if it were to be ratified by all of the remaining signatories—because its entry-into-force threshold[21] required that the agreement be ratified by six countries whose aggregate GDP was at least 85 percent of the aggregate GDP of all signatories.

Following the withdrawal by the US, the other 11 signatories removed the aggregate GDP requirement from the entry-into-force threshold, suspended or changed 22 provisions that had been introduced by the US, and renamed the instrument the "Comprehensive and Progressive Agreement for Trans-Pacific Partnership" (CPTPP). The CPTPP Agreement was signed in Santiago, Chile, in March 2018, and entered into force on December 30, 2018.

9.2.2   Operational Advantages of RTBs

Geographical proximity, focus, smaller size, and relative compatibility are operational advantages for all RIAs. In RTBs, these factors can facilitate better communication between members; reduce the range of members' political, social, cultural, and/or economic-development differences;

---

[21] Entry-into-force thresholds are discussed in Chapter 7, Section 7.3.2.2.

improve inter-member communication; make it less difficult for members to achieve agreement on key issues; make it possible to find solutions that are acceptable to all members; lead to the adoption of mutually agreeable decisions; and can improve the implementation and effectiveness of decisions.

RCEP Agreement

Article 10.3: National Treatment, of the RCEP Agreement,[22] says that RCEP members must accord foreign direct investors "treatment no less favorable than it accords … its own investors and their investments with respect to the establishment, acquisition, expansion, management, conduct, operation, and sale or other deposition of investments in its territory." This RCEP Agreement language is similar to the TRIMs Singapore Issue language—to which developing countries had objected at and following the WTO Ministerial Conference in Singapore.[23] The fact that two-thirds of the signatories to the RCEP Agreement are developing countries, and that all of these developing country governments agreed to be bound by the National Treatment provisions contained in Article 10.3 of the RCEP Agreement— is testimony to the operational distinctions between global and regional instruments and mechanisms, and to the extraordinary operational effectiveness of RTBs.

Most RTBs, like most global mechanisms, use some form of consensus decision-making.[24] For example, Article 14: Decision-Making, of the AfCFTA Agreement[25] says, "Decisions of the AfCFTA institutions on substantive issues shall be taken by consensus." But because the difficulty of finding a solution and/or language that is acceptable to all parties

---

[22] The RCEP Agreement is discussed in Section 7.3.2.1.

[23] The objections by developing countries to the TRIMs Singapore Issue is discussed in Chapter 8, Section 8.5.3.2.

[24] The use of consensus decision-making by the WTO is discussed in Chapter 8, Section 8.5.1.2.

[25] The AfCFTA Agreement is discussed in Chapter 7, Section 7.5.

increases exponentially with the number of participants in the process, the use of consensus decision-making by RTBs is generally less problematic than it is for global mechanisms.[26]

9.2.3 Extension of the Geographical Criterion

The word *regional* in the term *regional integration* indicates that the integration is by countries that are located in the same geographical region; and this geographical meaning also originally applied to the term *regional trade block*. But in RTBs, the term *regional* has been extended to apply to free trade areas that include participation by countries that are not from the same geographical region. For example, the GCC–Singapore[27] and the US–Singapore FTAs include countries from different geographical regions; and in 2023, the UK became a member of the Comprehensive and Progressive Agreement for Trans-Pacific Partnership (CPTPP)[28]— which extended participation in the CPTPP to a country that is not located within the Pacific Rim geographical region.

The use of the term *regional trade block* has also been extended, in some cases, by replacing the geographical integration criterion with an industry integration criterion.

DEPA

The "Digital Economy Partnership Agreement" (DEPA) was created by Chile, New Zealand, and Singapore; and came into effect in 2020. The purpose of this RTB is to facilitate trade and create a framework for the digital economy, increase exports of digital products and services, establish enterprise-friendly regulations that promote the member countries as digital economy platforms, and facilitate the exploration of new technological areas that can help society as a whole through inclusive economic development.

---

[26] This is also discussed in Section 9.5.1.
[27] The GCC–Singapore FTA is discussed in Chapter 7, Section 7.3.2.1.
[28] The CPTPP Agreement is discussed in Section 9.2.1.3.

9.2.4   Free Trade Areas and Customs Unions

Article XXIV, paragraph 5, of the GATT classifies all regional trade blocks as either free trade areas (FTAs) or customs unions (CUs). Because FTAs and CUs are not subject to approval by WTO members, they are referred to as "outside" agreements—but Article XXIV, paragraph 7.(a), requires that WTO members who are entering into an FTA or CU must notify the WTO regarding their intention, and provide related information.

The primary purpose of both FTAs and CUs is to facilitate trade by reducing or eliminating trade barriers between their member states. The differences between FTAs and CUs are structural and operational. The structural difference is that FTAs and CUs have significantly different levels of integration. The operational differences relate to the setting of external tariff barriers, NTBs, and other barriers to trade—and external trade policy.

9.3   Free Trade Areas

Article XXIV, paragraph 8(b), of the GATT says:

> A free-trade area [sic] shall be understood to mean a group of two or more customs territories[29] in which the duties and other restrictive regulations of commerce … are eliminated on substantially all the trade between the constituent territories in products originating in such territories.

Free trade areas are relatively limited integration RTBs: they require their member states to surrender relatively small amounts of their trade-related sovereignty.[30] Free trade areas include multilateral FTAs and bilateral FTAs. Multilateral FTAs are discussed in this section. Bilateral FTAs are discussed in Section 9.5.3.

---

[29] As discussed in Chapter 7, Section 7.1.3, the GATT uses the terms *country* and *customs territory* interchangeably.

[30] The partial surrender of sovereignty is discussed in Chapter 7, Section 7.1.5.3.

9.3.1   The Meaning and Use of the Term

The term *free trade area* does not mean that trade within an FTA is free—it does not mean there are no tariff barriers, non-tariff barriers, and/or other barriers to trade between the member countries of an FTA. Because Article XXIV.8(b) refers to the elimination of "substantially all" of the "duties and other restrictive regulations of commerce" between the member countries of an FTA, this has been taken to mean that the purpose and intent of an FTA is to reduce and substantially eliminate intramural barriers to trade between FTA member countries.

The RCEP Agreement

Article 1.1 of the RCEP Agreement says, "The Parties hereby establish" the RCEP "as a free trade area." Paragraph (1) of Article 2.4: Reduction or Elimination of Customs Duties, states that "each Party shall reduce or eliminate its customs on originating goods of other Parties."

The AfCFTA

Article 3 of the AfCFTA Agreement[31] says: "The general objectives of the AfCFTA are to ... create a liberalized market for goods and services through successive rounds of negotiations." Article 4 says that State Parties to the agreement should "(a) progressively eliminate tariffs and non-tariff barriers to trade in goods" and "(b) progressively liberalize trade in services." The AU website says: "It has been agreed that there should be 90% tariff liberalization. Over a 10 year period with a 5 year transition, there will be an additional 7% for 'sensitive products' that must be liberalized. This will be supported by the AfCFTA Trade in Goods online portal where Member States will upload their tariff offers covering 90% of the tariff lines."[32]

The "reduce or eliminate" provisions contained in the RCEP Agreement, and the "progressively eliminate" and "progressively liberalize"

---

[31] The AfCFTA Agreement is discussed in Chapter 7, Section 7.5.

[32] African Union, The African Continental Free Trade Area, website. The Tariff concessions.

provisions contained in the AfCFTA agreement, are consistent with the generally accepted interpretation of the "substantially all" language contained in Article XXIV.8(b) of the GATT.

The meaning of the initialism FTA can be ambiguous,[33] because it is commonly used when referring to either a free trade agreement and/or to a free trade area. To avoid this ambiguity, this book uses the initialism PTA (preferential trade agreement) when referring to the agreement that has created a free trade area; and uses the initialism FTA when referring to the free trade area that has been created by a PTA. This usage of the initialism FTA is consistent with the terms used in the GATT and by the WTO. For example, the GATT does not include any references to free trade agreement(s), but includes 15 references to free trade area(s).

9.3.2 *FTAs and MFN*

The language contained in Article XXIV, paragraph 8(b) of the GATT provides for the substantial elimination of "duties and other restrictive regulations of commerce" between two or more WTO members— without granting these same preferences to all other WTO members. This provision would appear to contradict the most-favored-nation require-ment contained in Article I of the GATT, which provides that "with respect to customs duties … any advantage, favor, privilege or immunity" granted to any WTO member must be granted to all WTO members.[34] This apparent contradiction is addressed by what is commonly referred to as the *Article XXIV exception*, which is seen as applying to all RTBs that have been notified to the WTO, including bilateral FTAs.[35]

The Article XXIV exception is based on the language contained in paragraphs 5 to 8 of Article XXIV, and especially paragraph 5, which says: "Accordingly, the provisions of this Agreement shall not prevent, as between the territories of contracting parties, the formation of a cus-toms union or of a free trade area …" The "exception" interpretation of these parts of Article XXIV has been supported by a 1999 Appellate Body

---

[33] PTAs and initialism ambiguity are discussed in Chapter 7, Section 7.1.6.

[34] The MFN requirement is discussed in Chapter 8, Section 8.4.1.

[35] Bilateral RTBs are discussed in Section 9.5.3.

report, which cited the position taken in a 1993 GATT panel report, that "Article XXIV: 5 to 8, permitted the contracting parties to deviate from their obligations under other provisions of the General Agreement"—and argued that "legal scholars have long considered Article XXIV to be an 'exception' or a possible 'defense' to claims of violations of GATT provisions."[36]

NAFTA

Following the implementation of the tariff phase-out provisions contained in the "North American Free Trade Agreement," "the US simple average tariff applied to imports from Mexico declined from 4.01 percent in 1989 ... to 0.52 percent in 2001."[37] The members of NAFTA were not required to extend these tariff phase-out provisions to all WTO members, because these preferences were between members of an RTB that had been notified to the WTO.[38]

The "Understanding on the Interpretation of Article XXIV of the General Agreement on Tariffs and Trade 1994," which is one of the Uruguay Round instruments,[39] does not specifically address the issue of FTAs and the MFN requirement—but this instrument is seen as confirming the Article XXIV exception.

9.3.3   FTA Trade Barriers and Policies

In the operation of free trade areas, there is an important distinction between the regulation of internal and external tariffs, NTBs, other barriers to trade, and trade policies.

---

[36] Appellate Body Report, Turkey—Restrictions on Imports of Textile and Clothing Products.

[37] Agama and McDaniel. n.d. "NAFTA and US–Mexico Trade."

[38] As discussed in Section 9.2.1.1, in 2020 the NAFTA was revised and renamed the USMCA.

[39] This instrument is also called the "Uruguay Round Understanding on the Interpretation of Article XXIV," or simply the "1994 Understanding." Uruguay Round instruments are discussed in Chapter 8, Section 8.4.3.2.

9.3.3.1   Internal Trade Barriers and Policies

A free trade area's internal trade barriers and policies are common. FTA member states have transferred to the FTA their sovereign authority to set tariff rates; to regulate the use of NTBs and other barriers to trade; and to establish and implement preferential rules of origin[40] and other trade policies—with the other members of their FTA.

In free trade areas, the common internal tariffs are called *preferential tariffs*.[41] In most FTAs, the preferential tariffs are extremely low or zero.

The ASEAN FTA: Shoes within the FTA
Within the ASEAN FTA, the preferential tariff on shoes is zero—if their country of origin is an ASEAN FTA member state.

9.3.3.2   External Trade Barriers and Policies

A free trade area's external trade barriers (including tariff rates, NTBs, and other barriers to trade) and external trade policies are not common. Each FTA member country has retained its sovereign authority to set tariff rates, NTBs, other barriers to trade, and trade policies with countries that are not members of its FTA.

The ASEAN FTA: External tariffs on shoes
Each member of the ASEAN FTA sets the tariff rate on shoes from countries that are not members of the ASEAN FTA. The tariff on shoes entering Thailand from outside the ASEAN FTA is 30 percent. The tariff on shoes entering Singapore from outside the FTA is zero.

The China–ASEAN FTA
Because an FTAs external trade tariffs, NTB, other barriers to trade, and trade policies are not common, when China was negotiating the China–ASEAN Free Trade Area it was necessary for China to negotiate a separate agreement with each ASEAN member state.

---

[40] Preferential rules of origin are discussed in Section 9.3.3.3.
[41] Preferential tariffs are discussed in Chapter 2, Section 2.1.6; and Chapter 7, Section 7.1.6.

The absence of common external trade barriers and trade policies can be problematic when a product from outside an FTA enters through a member state that has a low external tariff, and is then transshipped to a member state that has a higher external tariff.

The ASEAN FTA: The transshipment of shoes
   A manufacturer from outside the ASEAN FTA could try to avoid paying Thailand's 30 percent tariff on shoes—by importing shoes into Singapore (paying zero tariff), and then transshipping the shoes to Thailand.

9.3.3.3   Preferential Rules of Origin

Free trade areas try to control this transshipment problem by establishing and implementing rules of origin. As discussed in Chapter 2,[42] ROO are divided into two categories: preferential and non-preferential. Preferential rules of origin apply to trade between members of an FTA. Non-preferential ROO apply to trade between countries that are not members of the same FTA.

Some aspects of preferential and non-preferential rules of origin are the same. The purpose of both categories is to provide criteria that are used to determine a product's country of origin. In both cases, the term *country of origin* does not refer to the country from where a product was exported, but refers to the country where a product was produced or manufactured.

The principal differences between the two ROO categories are that preferential ROO:

1. Apply to trade between members of an FTA;
2. Are not covered by the Kyoto Convention or the "Agreement on Rules of Origin"[43];
3. Are set and enforced by the members of each FTA;

---

[42] See Chapter 2, Section 2.4.1.
[43] This agreement is discussed in Chapter 2, Section 2.4.2.

4. Often use a more complex set of criteria than non-preferential ROO; and

5. Frequently include criteria relating to the country of origin of the materials and components used in a product's production or manufacture.

9.3.3.4   Substantial Transformation

The substantial transformation criterion,[44] which is used when determining non-preferential country of origin, is also used by most FTAs; and the three methods for determining substantial transformation that are used to determine non-preferential country of origin are also used by FTAs. Some FTAs modify one of the three methods or combine elements from different methods.

The ASEAN FTA: The value-added method

When determining what constitutes a substantial transformation, the ROO for the ASEAN FTA use the value-added method.[45]

A product is eligible for ASEAN preferential treatment if "the total value of the materials, parts or produce originating from non-ASEAN countries or of undetermined origin used does not exceed 60% of the FOB value of the product produced or obtained and the final process of the manufacture is performed within the territory of the exporting Member State" or if "the aggregate ASEAN content of the final product is not less than 40%."[46]

USMCA: The change-in-tariff-classification method

The USMCA Rules of Origin are contained in Chapter 4 of the agreement. The USMCA ROO are based on the HS codes[47]

---

[44] The substantial transformation criterion is discussed in Chapter 2, Section 2.4.3.

[45] The value-added method for determining substantial transformation is discussed in Chapter 2, Section 2.4.3.

[46] ASEAN, Operational Certification Procedures, Article 3, Origin Criteria, (ii) and (iii).

[47] HS codes are discussed in Chapter 2, Section 2.3.1.

contained in the Harmonized Tariff Schedule of the US Annotated (HTSUSA), and use the change-in-tariff-classification method[48] (which is also called the tariff-shift method) when determining substantial transformation. In the USMCA ROO, however, the change-in-tariff-classification method is combined with product-specific local-content criteria, which (with some exceptions) limit the adjusted value of all non-originating materials (that is, materials that do not originate in one of the USMCA member countries) used in the production of a product to 10 percent of either the adjusted transaction value of the product, or the total cost of the product.

9.3.3.5   Transshipments Within an FTA

A free trade area's preferential tariffs apply only to products originating within the FTA. If products that do not comply with an FTA's ROO are transshipped within the FTA, they are subject to tariffs as if they were being imported from outside the FTA.

> The ASEAN FTA: The transshipment of shoes
> If shoes from outside the ASEAN FTA enter Singapore at no tariff and are transshipped to Thailand, they will be subject to 30 percent tariff when entering Thailand.

In some cases, the administration and enforcement of ROO is made more complex and difficult because of the use of false labeling.

9.3.4   Logistical Support

Free trade areas can be either functional mechanisms or organizational mechanisms.[49] FTAs that are closer to the limitedintegration end of the

---

[48] The change-in-tariff-classification method is discussed in Chapter 2, Section 2.4.3.
[49] Organizational and functional mechanisms are discussed in Chapter 7, Sections 7.4.2 and 7.4.3.

integration continuum[50] are more likely to be functional mechanisms. FTAs that are closer to the deep-integration end of the continuum, or are moving toward the deep-integration end of the continuum, are more likely to be organizational mechanisms.

USMCA

The USMCA is a functional mechanism: its logistical support is provided by departments or agencies of the governments of its member countries. Chapter 30, Administrative and Institutional Provisions, Article 30.1, establishes a Free Trade Commission, "composed of government representatives of each Party at the level of Ministers and their designees." Article 30.6 establishes a secretariat that is divided into three sections, one for each member country, with each member country designating "an individual to serve as Secretary for its Section."

9.4   Customs Unions

Article XXIV, paragraph 8(a), of the GATT says:

A customs union shall be understood to mean the substitution of a single customs territory for two or more customs territories, so that

(i) duties and other restrictive regulations of commerce ... are eliminated with respect to substantially all the trade between the constituent territories of the union or at least with respect to substantially all the trade in products originating in such territories, and,

(ii) ... substantially the same duties and other regulations of commerce are applied by each of the members of the union to the trade of territories not included in the union.

The language in part (i) of this text is the same as in Article XXIV, paragraph 8(b), which defines FTAs. This says that customs unions,

---

[50] Levels of integration are discussed in Section 9.1.2.

like free trade areas, have common internal policies and tariffs. The language that comes before and after part (i) of paragraph 8(a), defines the very significant structural and operational differences between FTAs and CUs.

9.4.1   The Primary Structural Difference

Article XXIV, paragraph 2, of the GATT says: "... a customs territory shall be understood to mean any territory with respect to which separate tariffs or other regulations of commerce are maintained for a substantial part of the trade of such territory with other territories." Because this definition applies to countries, the GATT uses the terms *country* and *customs territory* interchangeably.

Article XXIV, paragraph 8(b), says that an FTA is "a group of two or more customs territories." The first phrase of Article XXIV, paragraph 8(a), says a CU is the "substitution of a single customs territory for two or more customs territories."

This difference between FTAs and CUs is structural. An FTA facilitates trade between two or more customs territories by substantially eliminating trade barriers. A CU facilitates trade by replacing two or more customs territories with a new single customs territory. That is, CUs facilitate trade by placing the members of the CU in the same customs territory.

Because Article XII of the GATT defines a separate customs territory as an entity "possessing full autonomy in the conduct of its external commercial relations," and because CUs have common external tariff rates, NTBs, other barriers to trade, and trade policies—CUs are seen as complying with the definition of a separate customs territory. Based on the language contained in Article XXIV, paragraph 8(b), a CU can be referred to as a *single customs territory*. Based on the language contained in Article XII, CUs are also called *separate customs territories*.

Because membership in the WTO is limited to countries (which are customs territories) and separate customs territories, membership in the WTO is not open to FTAs, but is open to CUs. In 1995, the European Union was accepted as a member of the WTO. In the future, other CUs could become members of the WTO.

9.4.2   *The Primary Operational Difference*

The primary operational difference between FTAs and CUs is contained in part (ii) of Article XXIV, paragraph 8(b) of the GATT.

In an FTA, the member states have transferred to the FTA their sovereign authority over trade barriers and trade policies with other members of their FTA; which results in the members of FTAs having common internal tariff rates, NTBs, other barriers to trade; and having common internal trade policies. But each member of an FTA has retained its sovereign authority to set its own trade barriers and trade policies with countries that are not members of their FTA.

In a CU, the member states have transferred to the CU their sovereign authority over trade barriers and trade policies with other members of their CU—and with countries that are not members of their CU. This results in the members of CUs having common internal and external tariff rates, NTBs, other barriers to trade; and having common internal and external trade policies.

Because CUs have common external tariff rates, NTBs, other barriers to trade, and external trade policies—all members of a CU apply the "same duties and other regulations of commerce" to countries that are not members of the CU.

GCC

In 2003, the GCC FTA became a customs union. The GCC's Supreme Council abolished all "customs duties .... regulations and procedures restricting trade among the member States" and implemented "unified customs duties ... and trade and customs regulations for trade with non-member States."[51]

The EU

The first two paragraphs of Part One, Article 3, of the "Treaty of Rome" (1957), state that it is the intention of the parties to: (a) eliminate customs duties on "the importation and exportation of goods, as well as all other measures with equivalent effect,"

---

[51] GCC, Implementation Procedures.

between the member states; and (b) to establish "a common customs tariff and a common commercial policy towards third countries."[52] These provisions of the "Treaty of Rome" came into full effect in 1986, with the adoption of the "Single European Act" by the European Parliament, and were confirmed in 1992 by the provisions contained in the "Maastricht Treaty."[53]

If the "Treaty of Rome" had included Part One, Article 3, paragraph (a), but had not included paragraph (b), then the EU would have been an FTA. But because paragraph (b) provides for "the establishment of a common customs tariff and a common commercial policy towards third countries," the EU is a customs union.[54]

The member states of the EU have transferred their sovereign authority over internal and external trade barriers and policies to the EU. The EU sets the tariff rates (and regulates the use of NTBs and other barriers to trade) on all products entering and leaving the EU; establishes and implements the EU's internal and external trade policies, which include the rules of origin that are applied to products entering the EU; and represents the EU member states in trade negotiations with other nation-states.

The EAEU

The name and functions of the Eurasian Economic Union (EAEU), like the name and functions of the European Union, have evolved.[55] In 2000, five members of the CIS[56] (which was founded as an RIA following the dissolution of the Soviet Union in 1991) created the Eurasian Economic Community (EAEC or EurAsEC),

---

[52] Part One—Principles, Article 3, paragraphs (a) and (b), "Treaty Establishing the European Economic Community."

[53] The "Treaty of Rome," the "Single European Act," and the "Maastricht Treaty"—and their roles in European regional integration—are discussed in Section 9.2.1.2.

[54] The "Treaty of Rome" provisions for the establishment of the EU as a customs union are contained in Part Two—Bases of the Community; Title I—Free Movement of Goods; Chapter 1—The Customs Union.

[55] The origins and evolution of the EU is discussed in Section 9.2.1.2.

[56] Belarus, Kazakhstan, Kyrgyzstan, Russia, and Tajikistan.

which functioned as an FTA. In 2010, the EAEC became the Eurasian Customs Union (EACU), and Kyrgyzstan and Tajikistan chose to leave the organization. In 2011, the members of the EACU created a secretariat, which is called the Eurasian Economic Commission (EEC); and adopted the Customs Code of the Eurasian Customs Union (ECU-CC), which provided for common external trade barriers and policies—and caused the organization to change from being an FTA to being a CU.[57]

In 2014, the members of the EACU entered into the "Treaty on the Eurasian Economic Union," which came into effect on January 1, 2015, and created the EAEU. In 2015, Armenia and Kyrgyzstan[58] became members of the EAEU.[59] The "Treaty on the Eurasian Economic Union," Article 2: Definitions, says a customs union is "a form of trade and economic integration of the member States that provides for a unified customs territory free from customs duties [and] non-tariff measures, ... but with common customs tariff and common assessment methods regulating foreign trade with third parties."

The operationalization of the provisions contained in part (ii) of Article XXIV, paragraph 8(b) of the GATT causes the members and non-members of a CU to see and treat the CU as a single customs territory—which is why a CU is referred to as "a single market" or "a common market." The names of CUs can include the word *community*, *union*, or *common market*.

Customs unions include:

- Andean Community (CAN)
- East Africa Community (EAC)
- Eurasian Economic Union (EAEU)
- European Union (EU)
- Gulf Cooperation Council (GCC)

---

[57] The founding members of the EACU were Belarus, Kazakhstan, and Russia.
[58] Kyrgyzstan had previously been a member of the EAEC.
[59] The members of the EAEU are Armenia, Belarus, Kazakhstan, Kyrgyzstan, and Russia.

- Southern African Customs Union (SACU)
- Southern Common Market (SCM)

Several RTBs are working toward becoming customs unions. These prospective CUs include: the African Economic Community, the Arab Customs Union, the Central American Common Market, the Economic Community of West African States, and the Union of South American Nations.

9.4.3   CUs and the Partial Surrender of Sovereignty

Customs unions are relatively deep-integration RTBs:[60] As a general rule, CUs require their member states to surrender all of the trade-related parts of their sovereignty to the CU.[61]

The EAEU

The "Treaty on the Eurasian Economic Union," Section IX: Foreign Trade Policy, says that the EAEU's "Foreign trade policy is implemented by conclusion of international treaties with third parties, unilaterally by the EAEU or jointly with the member States, in the spheres where the EAEU's bodies take decisions, which are mandatory for the member States."

The EFTA

The European Free Trade Association (EFTA) is an FTA that includes Iceland, Liechtenstein, Norway, and Switzerland, which was created in 1960 for European countries that are averse to the partial surrender of sovereignty that is required by membership in a customs union.

Because customs union members have transferred to the CU the trade-related parts of their sovereignty, which include their trade-related regulatory authority—they no longer have the authority to set their own

---

[60] Levels of regional integration are discussed in Section 9.1.2.

[61] The partial surrender of sovereignty is discussed in Chapter 7, Section 7.1.5.3.

tariff rates, create and apply their own NTBs and other barriers to trade, or enter into bilateral or multilateral trade agreements.

The EU and Canada

The "Canada–EU Comprehensive Economic and Trade Agreement"[62] (CETA) is a bilateral FTA[63] between a country and a separate customs territory. Because the European Union is a CU, this agreement was entered into by the EU per se, and not by the members of the EU.

The EAEU

When the Eurasian Economic Community became the Eurasian Customs Union, which foreshadowed its adoption of the Customs Code of the Eurasian Customs Union and its change from being an FTA to being a CU—Kyrgyzstan and Tajikistan left the organization.[64] The decisions by these countries to leave were driven by their not wanting to surrender additional trade-related parts of their sovereignty.[65]

9.4.4 Transshipments Within CUs

The country of origin issue, which is problematic for transshipments within FTAs, does not present a problem in customs unions. Because CUs have common internal and external trade barriers and policies, all CU member states apply the same tariff rates to a product category entering their CU. Once a product has entered the CU, it is treated the same as products that are produced or manufactured within the CU.

---

[62] The CETA is discussed in Chapter 3, Section 3.3.2.2.

[63] Bilateral RTBs are discussed in Section 9.5.3.

[64] This is discussed in the EAEU example, in Section 9.4.2.

[65] In 2015, Kyrgyzstan rejoined the organization, by when it had become the EAEU.

The EU: The transshipment of shoes

The tariff on shoes from outside the European Union entering France, Spain, Italy, or any other EU member state is 8 percent. Once shoes from outside the FTA have entered the EU, and have paid the common EU tariff, they may be transshipped to any other EU member state without paying any additional customs duties.

Because products that have entered a CU receive the same treatment as products that are produced or manufactured within the CU, the transshipments of products within a CU does not involve the application of preferential rules of origin.[66] The only use of rules of origin by CUs is the application of non-preferential rules of origin[67] on products that are imported into the CU.

The EAEU

The "Treaty on the Eurasian Economic Union,"[68] Article 37: Rules for Determination of the Origin of Goods, says that, for "goods imported into the customs territory of the EAEU, ... non-preferential rules for determination of the origin of goods shall be applied."

Although customs unions have the advantage of avoiding the country of origin problems that are associated with transshipments within FTAs, this advantage comes at a price. Because the member states of CUs have given up their sovereign authority to set trade barriers and make trade policy, they no longer have the authority to individually apply trade-related measures to protect their country's products, companies, industries, and jobs.

---

[66] Preferential rules of origin are discussed in Chapter 2, Section 2.4; and Section 9.3.3 of this chapter.

[67] Non-preferential rules of origin are discussed in Chapter 2, Section 2.4.

[68] The "Treaty on the Eurasian Economic Union" is discussed in Section 9.4.2.

Italy, Spain, France, and Germany: Shoes, prices, and protection

The European Union has set a low tariff on shoes, which benefits the consumers in member states by avoiding duties that would add significantly to the price of imported shoes. But this low tariff has an adverse effect on shoe and leather industry manufacturers, suppliers, and employees in the EU—and especially on those in the large shoe and leather industries in Italy, Spain, France, and Germany. Because the governments of Italy, Spain, France, and Germany (and other EU countries) have given up the trade-related parts of their sovereignty, they are no longer able to apply country-specific trade barriers to protect their shoe and leather industries, and to protect their nationals who work in their shoe and leather industries.

9.4.5 *Varying Levels of CU Integration*

Compared to free trade areas, CUs have more unified trade barriers and trade policies, and all customs unions are deep-integration RTBs. But not all CUs have the same level of integration. External trade barriers and trade policies are less unified in some CUs,[69] and in some CUs different member states have different external trade quotas.

Because the European Union began with the "Treaty of Rome" and the creation of the EEC in 1957, and because the EU is the most deeply integrated CU, a CU's depth of integration is sometimes seen as being a function of its age. But, in most cases, the factor that determines a CU's level of integration is the degree to which its member countries are prepared to surrender more of their trade-relate sovereignty.

Whereas most FTAs are functional mechanisms, all CUs are organizational mechanisms. The most developed of these is the EU's organizational mechanisms, which includes a political body, a legislative body, and an executive body—which is larger and more developed

---

[69] For example, two GCC CU member states (Bahrain and Oman) have entered into separate bilateral trade agreements (with the United States).

than the executive branches of the governments of some developed countries.[70]

9.5   Bilateral Instruments and Mechanisms

In the field of international relations, the term *bilateral* indicates participation by two nation-states. In the field of international commerce, the term *bilateral* also includes participation by separate customs territories, which can include: (1) participation by a nation-state and a separate customs territory, or (2) participation by two separate customs territories.[71]

9.5.1   Bilateral Instruments

The bilateral instrument is the workhorse of international trade and FDI facilitation. The GATT and other WTO instruments, and non-WTO global instruments, prescribe the concepts, principles, rules, requirements, legal frameworks, and operational provisions that govern the conduct of international trade and FDI. Regional PTAs (and the RTBs they create) facilitate regional integration and economic development by reducing or eliminating interregional barriers to trade and FDI. Bilateral trade and FDI instruments facilitate the conduct of bilateral international commerce by specifying the terms and conditions that govern trade and FDI between two nation-states, and by reducing or removing barriers to trade and FDI between two nation-states.

Bilateral trade and FDI agreements are more narrowly focused than global and regional agreements; and because the complexity of all agreements tends to increase exponentially with the addition of each participant—bilateral trade and FDI agreements are less complex than global and regional agreements. These characteristics can facilitate the initiation, negotiation, drafting, signing, ratification, and implementation of bilateral instruments.

---

[70] Some elements of the EU's organizational mechanism are discussed in Section 9.2.1.2.

[71] Separate customs territories are discussed in Chapter 7, Section 7.1.3.

The US: Bilateral instruments

The Office of the United States Trade Representative (USTR) says that US trade agreements include: 20 Free Trade Agreements (FTAs) and Trade Promotion Agreements (TPAs), of which 12 are bilateral FTAs or TPAs; more than 40 Bilateral Investment Treaties (BITs); and more than 50 Trade and Investment Framework Agreements (TIFAs), almost all of which are bilateral agreements.

9.5.2   Bilateral Mechanisms

There are several structural and operational factors that differentiate bilateral trade and FDI mechanisms from global and regional mechanisms. These factors include size, specificity, efficiency, and control.

9.5.2.1   Compared to Global Mechanisms

The most conspicuous structural factor that differentiates bilateral trade and FDI mechanisms from global mechanisms is their size. The reason for the failure of the Doha Round of multilateral trade negotiations was due in part to the North–South divisions over issues[72]—but the reason for the failure was also structural: the Doha Round of trade negotiations involved participation by more than 150 parties.

9.5.2.2   Compared to Regional Mechanisms

As discussed in Section 9.2.2, the size, proximity, focus, and compatibility characteristics of regional trade and FDI mechanisms can reduce the range of their members' political, social, cultural, and/or economic-development differences; improve their members' relative compatibility; improve inter-member communication; make it less difficult for members to achieve agreement on key issues; make it possible to find solutions

---

[72] The failure of the Doha Round and the North–South divisions over issues are discussed in Chapter 8, Sections 8.5.3.1 and 8.6; and in the "WTO operational issues" supplemental reading.

that are acceptable to all members; and can improve the implementation and effectiveness of decisions. But although multilateral RTBs are significantly smaller than global trade and FDI mechanisms, the size of multilateral RTBs can still be problematic.

The UK: Withdrawal from the EU

The United Kingdom acceded to membership in the European Economic Community[73] in 1973. In March 2017, the UK notified the European Union of its intention to withdraw; and on January 31, 2020, the UK's withdrawal from the EU came into effect. One of the reasons for the UK's withdrawal from the EU was the perception within the UK that the organizational administration of the EU is so large, bureaucratic, and unwieldy that it has become a law unto itself—and that this prevents the EU from acting in the interest of its individual member states.

9.5.2.3   Specificity, Efficiency, and Control

A second structural factor that differentiates bilateral mechanisms is their specificity. The parties to bilateral agreements can choose to address only those international trade and/or FDI issues that are of immediate concern to them—and in each case to choose the specific form and structure that they believe will best effect the implementation and administration of an agreement.

A third structural difference is that all global trade mechanisms and many multilateral RTBs are organizational mechanisms[74]—which have a secretariat, an administrative and operational structure, officers, employees, and physical facilities. The logistical support for the implementation and administration of bilateral trade agreements, however, is through functional mechanisms[75]—which are provided by the

---

[73] The European Economic Community (EEC) is discussed in Section 9.2.1.2. In 1993, the EEC was renamed the European Community, and was incorporated as a founding element of the European Union.

[74] Organizational mechanisms are discussed in Chapter 7, Section 7.4.2.

[75] Functional mechanisms are discussed in Chapter 7, Section 7.4.3.

government departments and/or agencies of the two countries that are parties to the agreement. This structural difference makes bilateral trade and FDI mechanisms efficient and effective, and allows the parties to bilateral agreements to retain control over the interpretation and implementation of the terms of agreements.

And, finally, as discussed in Sections 9.3 and 9.4, countries that have entered into multilateral RTB agreements, including both FTA and CU agreements, have transferred to the organization and its administrative mechanism parts or all of their trade-related and FDI-related sovereignty, and have surrendered control over some or all of their trade-related and FDI-related decision-making authority.

The UK: Withdrawal from the EU

One of the reasons that prompted the UK to withdraw from the EU was the perception that the organizational administration of the EU had become a law unto itself. But the UK's withdrawal from the EU was also about sovereignty: by leaving the EU, the UK was taking back control over the trade-related parts of its sovereignty.[76]

9.5.3   Bilateral FTAs and MFN

The most-favored-nation clause, which is contained in Article I of the GATT, requires that any preference granted to any WTO member must be "accorded immediately and unconditionally" to "all other members."[77] But, paragraphs 5 to 8, of Article XXIV of the GATT, are seen as exempting preferences between members of free trade areas from the MFN requirement. Because of the "two or more" language contained in Article XXIV, this exemption applies to bilateral FTAs.[78]

The exception contained in Article XXIV allows two countries to enter into a trade agreement, to notify their agreement to the WTO as a bilateral FTA, and to use this as the grounds for not having to comply with

---

[76] Sovereignty is discussed in Chapter 7, Section 7.1.5.

[77] This provision of the MFN clause is discussed in Chapter 8, Section 8.4.1.5.

[78] The Article XXIV exception is discussed in Chapter 9, Section 9.3.2.

the provisions of the MFN clause. This use of the Article XXIV exception has produced two tangible effects: (1) It has resulted in an attenuation in the application and effectiveness of the MFN requirement; and (2) it has contributed to the proliferation of PTAs and RTBs—and especially the proliferation of bilateral PTAs and bilateral FTAs.

CHAPTER 10

International Standards

Contents

10.1 Introduction

Differences in national product standards in different countries can mean that a component, product, or service that is produced in one country cannot be used in another country—which limits or prevents the international sale and purchase of the component, product, or service.

Differences in national product standards can, therefore, act as technical barriers to trade.[1]

10.1.1   The Need for National Standards

The reason national product standards were first developed, in the early 20th century, was to make it possible for components manufactured by one company to be used in the manufacture of components or products by another company, or to make it possible for a product manufactured by one company to be connected to and operated with products manufactured by other companies.

ANSI

In 1918, a group of five engineering and materials-testing societies in the United States formed a non-governmental organization called the American National Standards Institute (ANSI), which in 1919 developed a product standard relating to pipe threads. This product standard allowed pipes and pipe fittings manufactured by different companies to be interconnected and, therefore, to be used as fungible components in products and/or construction projects.

Over the next decade, ANSI approved national product standards in the fields of mining, electrical and mechanical engineering, construction, and highway traffic. In 1921, ANSI approved its first process standards. These standards were for the protection of the heads and eyes of industrial workers. There are now more than 230 ANSI-accredited Standard Development Organizations, and more than 11,500 American National Standards, which include both product standards and process standards.

National standards are developed and/or approved by industry organizations, national governments, governmental agencies, which are referred to as standards organizations. Standards organizations can be governmental or non-governmental, and can be national or international.

---

[1] Technical barriers to trade are discussed in Chapter 3, Section 3.2.

10.1.2 The Need for International Standards

The need for international trade-related standards is an extension of the need for national product standards. International standards facilitate the conduct of international trade by making it possible for components, products, and services that are produced in one country to be sold, purchased, and used in other countries.

The preamble to the 1994 "Agreement on Technical Barriers to Trade,"[2] says that the Members of the WTO recognize "the important contribution that international standards and conformity assessment systems can make … by improving [the] efficiency of production and [by] facilitating the conduct of international trade."

Haier

Haier is the largest manufacturer and marketer of home appliances in China, and holds the largest share of the global home appliance market. When Haier developed its internationalization strategy in 1998, it had its products tested and approved by Underwriters Laboratories Inc. (UL) and 14 other certifying organizations in 48 countries.

The "General Agreement on Trade in Services" (GATS)[3] says that WTO members "recognize the importance of international standards for global compatibility and inter-operability of telecommunications networks and services and undertake to promote such standards through the work of relevant international bodies, including the International Telecommunications Union and the International Organization of Standardization."[4]

The ITU

International Telecommunications Union (ITU) was created in 1865, to facilitate the establishment of an international telegraph

---

[2] The TBT agreement is discussed in Section 10.2.
[3] The GATS is discussed in Chapter 8, Sections 8.4.3.2, 8.5.3, and 8.5.3.1.
[4] GATS, Annex on Telecommunications, para 7(a).

network. The ITU is now a specialized agency of the UN, and includes 14 study groups that advise on standards.

10.2   The TBT Agreement

As discussed in Chapter 3, Article XX of the GATT[5] includes a list of general exceptions that allow WTO members to use specific non-tariff barriers (NTBs), which are referred to as *technical barriers to trade* (TBT).

In 1979, during the Tokyo Round of multilateral trade negotiations, 32 GATT contracting parties entered into the plurilateral[6] "Agreement on Technical Barriers to Trade," which is commonly referred to as the *Tokyo Round Standards Code.*[7] During the Uruguay Round,[8] the Tokyo Round Standards Code was revised and adopted as the multilateral 1994 "Agreement on Technical Barriers to Trade" (TBT agreement), which came into effect with the creation of the WTO on January 1, 1995.

The TBT agreement provides two categories of international standards: (1) *standards* and (2) *technical regulations. Standards*, which are voluntary, are defined as "rules, guidelines or characteristics for products or related processes and production methods."[9] *Technical regulations*, which are mandatory, are defined as "product characteristics or their related processes and production methods, including the applicable administrative provisions."[10] The TBT agreement says that both standards and technical regulations: "may also include or deal exclusively with terminology, symbols, packaging, marking or labeling requirements as they apply to a product, process or production method."[11]

These TBT agreement categories and definitions reflect the general practice of classifying international trade-related standards as either

---

[5] All references to the GATT that do not specify a year are to GATT 1994 (which includes GATT 1947). This is discussed in Chapter 8, Section 8.4.3.2.
[6] Plurilateral and multilateral agreements are discussed in Chapter 8, Section 8.4.3.3.
[7] The Tokyo Round is discussed in Chapter 8, Section 8.4.3.1.
[8] The Uruguay Round is discussed in Chapter 8, Section 8.4.3.2.
[9] Agreement on Technical Barriers to Trade, Annex I, 2. Standard.
[10] Agreement on Technical Barriers to Trade, Annex I, 1. Technical regulation.
[11] Agreement on Technical Barriers to Trade, Annex I, 1 and 2.

product or process standards, and as voluntary or mandatory standards. Product and process standards are discussed in Section 10.3; voluntary and mandatory standards are discussed in Section 10.4.

10.3   Product and Process Standards

The TBT agreement definition for *standards* refers to "rules, guidelines or characteristics for products or related processes and production methods." The TBT agreement definition for *technical regulations* refers to "product characteristics or their related processes and production methods, including the applicable administrative provisions."[12] These definitions reflect the general practice of referring to voluntary and mandatory trade-related standards as either (1) *product standards* or (2) *process standards*.

10.3.1   International Product Standards

Product standards cover the design, quality (which can include reliability), safety, performance (which can include serviceability), cost of operation, and/or durability of a product; the materials from which a product is made; and/or the possible adverse effects that the product may have on society. Product standards can be classified as design standards, quality standards, safety standards, performance standards, cost of operation standards, durability standards, materials standards, and social-responsibility standards. Product standards also include what are referred to as *conformity assessment procedures*, which include product testing, inspection, and certification.

10.3.1.1   ISO Product Standards

The oldest international standards organization is the International Electrotechnical Commission (IEC), which was established in 1906. The most influential international standards organization, and the world's largest developer of international standards, is the International Organization

---

[12] See Section 10.2.

for Standardization (ISO).[13] The ISO was created in 1946, by national standards organizations from 25 countries.

The ISO is a non-governmental organization, which is headquartered in Geneva (Switzerland). The ISO's membership is composed of one national standards organization from each member country, which can be a governmental or non-governmental organization. For example, the ISO members from Canada and China are the Standards Council of Canada (SCC) and the Standards Administration of China (SAC), which are governmental organizations; the ISO members from the UK and the US are the British Standards Institution (BSI) and ANSI, which are non-governmental organizations.

Since 1946, the ISO has developed more than 24,000 standards; currently covers all standards areas except those covered by the IEC; and includes more than 800 technical committees or subcommittees, and more than 3,600 technical bodies that develop standards. Until the mid-1990s, the ISO's primary focus was on product standards—which the ISO calls *technical standards*. These include standardized threads for pipes, nuts, and bolts; standardized paper sizes; and standardized dimensions and designs for freight containers.

Paper sizes

ISO technical standard ISO 216:2007 specifies the A4 letter size that is used in all countries except the United States and Canada. This product standard is used by thousands of companies in all parts of the world (including the US and Canada) that make and market paper, and that make and market products that are tied to these paper standards (such as word processing software, computer printers, copying machines, envelopes, folders, and binders).

Freight containers

The safe and effective international transportation of products in freight containers is possible only because companies in all parts of the world that design and manufacture freight containers, container ships, container trucks, and the cranes that stack and load

---

[13] The acronym ISO is not an abbreviation of the organization's name, but is derived from the Greek word "isos," which means "equal."

freight containers, use dimensions, designs, and safety standards that are covered by ISO technical standards.

Other international product standards organizations include more than 100 global alliances, associations, councils, consortiums, forums, foundations, groups, institutes, and unions; and more than 20 regional standards organizations.

10.3.1.2   Product Social-Responsibility Standards

Product social-responsibility standards include any aspect of a product, its use, or its post-use disposal that could cause harm to persons who are using the product, other persons, or any aspect of society or the physical environment. Physical environment product social-responsibility standards include motor vehicle safety and emissions standards, and standards for the disposal of electrical batteries.

Germany: Electrical tools

The example discussed in Chapter 3, Section 3.2.4, concerned the seizure of a large quantity of electrical tools on the grounds that these products contained a chemical carcinogen called PAH. If this action had been based on a German or EU standards relating to the content of PAH in electrical tools, this would have been a product social-responsibility standard.

The product social-responsibility standards that have historically received the most attention have been product safety standards—which cover the safety of the users of a product, but also cover the safety of a product to nonusers, to society, and to the physical environment.

The UL Mark

Underwriters Laboratories Inc. is an independent product-safety testing and certification organization, which was founded in the United States in 1895, has since then developed more than 1,400 safety-related standards, and every year performs more than 100,000 product evaluations at testing and certification facilities in 104 countries.

10.3.2   *International Process Standards*

The term *process standards* refers to a company's product-development processes, manufacturing processes, quality-management processes, human resources management processes, and environmental protection management processes.

10.3.2.1   ISO Process Standards

Since the mid-1990s, the focus of the ISO has been increasingly on process standards, which include its ISO 9000 and ISO 14000 families. The ISO 9000 family of standards, which ISO calls its *Quality Management Systems*, was originally developed in 1987. These process standards, which cover both products and services, are in use by over one million companies and organizations in over 170 countries. The ISO 14000 family of standards, which ISO calls its *Environmental Management Systems* and was originally developed in 1994, cover, inter alia, environmental audits, communications, labeling, life-cycle analysis, and climate change.

10.3.2.2   Other Process Standards

Process standards often affect and are reflected in the quality of products. It is important to note, however, that process standards govern the design, development, and manufacturing processes that are used when producing a product—rather than the design, quality, or other aspects of the product per se. For example, total quality management (TQM) and Six Sigma are process standards.

10.3.2.3   Process Social-Responsibility Standards

International process standards, like international product standards, can include international process social-responsibility standards. These standards cover the processes that are used in the manufacture of products; the use of materials and chemicals in manufacturing that can be potentially harmful to persons who are engaged in the production of a product, to other persons, to society, and/or to the physical environment; the disposal of waste materials and chemicals that have been used in manufacturing processes; and the processes, materials, and equipment that are used in agriculture.

The Wellington Convention

In 1989, 14 countries, which included the United States, signed the "Wellington Convention of the Prohibition of Fishing with Long Driftnets in the South Pacific," which prohibits fishing processes in the South Pacific that use fishing driftnets that are longer than 2.5 kilometers.

Code of Conduct for Responsible Fisheries

The 1995 Code of Conduct for Responsible Fisheries, which was created by the Food and Agriculture Organization of the United Nations, "sets out principles and international standards of behavior for responsible practices with a view to ensuring the effective conservation, management, and development of living aquatic resources, with due respect for the ecosystem and biodiversity. The Code recognizes the nutritional, economic, social, environmental, and cultural importance of fisheries and the interests of all those concerned with the fishery sector."[14]

10.4   Voluntary and Mandatory Standards

The TBT agreement definitions say that trade-related product and process standards are either voluntary or mandatory. Because non-governmental and intergovernmental organizations do not have the power to enact and enforce legislation and/or regulations that govern the behaviors of individuals and/or entities engaged in the practice of international trade and/or FDI—the international standards developed by these organizations are voluntary.[15] For example, the IEC and ISO are non-governmental organizations—and all of the standards developed by these organizations are voluntary standards.

---

[14] FOA. *Code of Conduct for Responsible Fisheries*, Introduction.
[15] An exception to this generalization is that in some cases the members of a nongovernmental industry organization have entered into a contractual commitment to comply with their industry organization's standards.

Because both non-governmental and intergovernmental organizations lack legislative or regulatory authority, most mandatory trade-related standards are those that are enacted and implemented by a nation-state. A standard developed by an intergovernmental organization can, however, become a mandatory standard of a nation-state: (1) if the standard is contained in an international agreement to which that nation-state is a party; and (2) if the provisions of that agreement become law in that nation-state, either automatically or through implementing legislation.

The US: Self-executing and non-self-executing agreements

In the United States, some international agreements are self-executing, which means that the provisions of an agreement "have the force of domestic law without the need for subsequent congressional action." In some cases, and especially where an agreement "text manifests an intent that the provision not be directly enforceable in U.S. courts," or where a provision "requires expenditure of funds" or "proport to criminal liability or raise revenue," these agreements may be deemed non-self-executing. The provisions of non-self-executing agreements do not have the force of domestic law until implementing legislation has been enacted.[16]

In some cases, the purpose of a standard enacted by a nation-state is primarily domestic, but because this standard also applies to imports, it becomes a trade-related standard. For example, when a country creates mandatory domestic motor vehicle safety and emissions standards, these standards also apply to motor vehicles that are being imported, which makes them mandatory trade-related standards.

There is a widely held view that, because individuals and entities engaged in the practice of international trade and/or FDI are not required to use voluntary standards, and because voluntary standards are not enforceable—voluntary standards are less effective than mandatory standards. But the wide use and extraordinary effectiveness of UL, ISO, IEC, and other voluntary standards has shown that the altruism and/or

---

[16] The quotations in this paragraph are from CRS, *International Law and Agreements*, p. 15.

rational self-interest that drives the adoption and implementation of voluntary standards can be as effective or, in many cases, more effective than enforceable mandatory standards.

One of the reasons for the extraordinary effectiveness of UL, ISO, IEC, and other voluntary standards is that many entities engaged in the practice of international trade and/or FDI require that their suppliers be certified in one or more designated voluntary standards. These requirements can have the effect of converting a voluntary standard into a mandatory contract-specific standard.

10.5   International Behavioral Standards

The social-responsibility principles that are applied in product and process standards have, since the 1950s, also been applied to the behaviors of entities that are engaged in the production and marketing of product and services—and in some cases to the individuals employed by those entities. This application of social-responsibility principles is generally referred to as *corporate social responsibility* (CSR). Like international product and process standards, international CSR standards are developed and propagated by non-governmental and intergovernmental organizations, and by the governments of individual nation-states;[17] and can be voluntary or mandatory.

10.5.1   Non-governmental CSR Standards

Non-governmental international CSR standards range from the general non-certification principles and definitions contained in ISO 26000 Guidance on Social Responsibility, to the specific outcomes-driven certification standards contained in the Fairtrade International Standards.

ISO 26000, Guidance on Social Responsibility
The ISO, which has tens of thousands of product and process standards, has only one behavioral standard, ISO 26000 Guidance

---

[17] International CSR standards are also included in company-specific FDI agreements, which are discussed in Chapter 6, Sections 6.2 and 6.3.

on Social Responsibility. This standard, which "is not a management system standard ... [and] is not intended for certification purposes," was adopted in 2010 and reviewed and confirmed in 2021; includes concepts, terms, and definitions relating to social responsibility; and provides guidance on "integrating, implementing, and promoting socially responsible behavior throughout the organization and ... its policies and practices."[18]

Fairtrade International Standards

Fairtrade International is an association of 22 member organizations, three producer networks, and 19 national Fairtrade organizations. It develops and propagates the Fairtrade Standards, which "are designed to tackle poverty and empower producers in the poorest countries in the world ... [and] include a range of economic, environmental, and social criteria that must be met by producers and traders in order to acquire or retain Fairtrade certification."[19]

Standards for small-scale producers cover the form of organization, transparency, decision-making, and non-discrimination; ecologically and agriculturally sound farming practices, which cover water and waste management, biodiversity and soil fertility, and the use of pesticides and agrochemicals; and prohibitions against forced labor and child labor. The standards for traders cover the payment of Fairtrade Minimum Price and a fixed Fairtrade Premium; long-term trading partnerships; and in some cases providing farmers with pre-financing and access to capital.

10.5.2   Intergovernmental CSR Standards

The TBT agreement, which defines and provides extensive information on international product and process standards, includes no information or standards concerning the behaviors of individuals and/or entities that are engaged in the practice of international trade and/or FDI. There

---

[18]   ISO 26000 Guidance on Social Responsibility.
[19]   Fairtrade International. About the standards.

are, however, many other intergovernmental agreements that have been deposited with the UN or notified to the WTO—that include provisions relating to the behaviors of individuals and entities engaged in the practice of international trade and/or FDI. Some of these agreements "refer explicitly to CSR,"[20] use other terms such as "responsible business conduct" that cover both individuals and entities, or use terms that address a specific corporate social-responsibility behavior or issue.

The 1976 OECD "Declaration on International Investment and Multinational Enterprises," contains the *OECD Guidelines for Multinational Enterprises*—which "provide non-binding principles and standards for responsible business conduct in a global context consistent with applicable laws and internationally recognized standards ... [and] are the only multilaterally agreed and comprehensive code of responsible business conduct that governments have committed to promoting." In 1997, the members of the OECD entered into an anti-bribery convention.

OECD Anti-Bribery Convention

The 1997 OECD "Convention on Combating Bribery of Foreign Public Officials in International Business Transactions," which came into effect in February 1999, provides that each of the nation-states that are parties to the convention shall make it "a criminal offence under its law for any person intentionally to offer, promise or giver any undue pecuniary or other advantage, whether directly or through intermediaries, to a foreign public official ... in order that the official act or refrain from acting in relation to the performance of official duties in order to obtain or retain business or other improper advantage in the conduct of international business."[21]

One of the factors that drive FDI can be an entity's interest in accessing labor at a lower cost than it is paying in its home country, or that it is paying in a host country where it is currently a foreign direct investor.

---

[20] Monteiro. 2021. Buena Vista: Corporate Social Responsibility Provisions in Regional Trade Agreements. WTO Economic Research and Statistics Division.
[21] OECD Anti-Bribery Convention. Article 1.1.

Because of this, employee working conditions and employee compensation have been and continue to be perennial international CSR issues.

The ILO: Minimum wage standards

The International Labor Organization (ILO) was established by Part XIII, Labor, of the 1919 "Treaty of Versailles"[22]—which addressed a range of working condition issues and "the payment to the employed of a wage adequate to maintain a reasonable standard of life as this is understood in their time and country."[23] Since then, working condition issues and minimum wage standards have been the focus of numerous ILO papers, reports, and conventions. Since 2008, the ILO has published a biennial Global Wage Report, some editions of which have focused on minimum wage policies and practices.

Other international instruments that have established international standards that cover working conditions and the payment of minimum wages have included: Article 23, paragraph 3, of the 1948 "Universal Declaration of Human Rights"; Article 7 of the 1966 "International Covenant on Economic, Social and Cultural Rights"; Article 5 of the "Community Charter" of the 1989 Fundamental Social Rights of Workers; Article II, paragraph 2(viii) of the 2004 "Social Charter of the South Asian Association for Regional Cooperation" (SAARC); and Article 34 of the 2004 "Arab Charter on Human Rights," which was adopted at the 16th Session of the Summit of the League of Arab States.[24]

Annex 1 of the 1993 "North American Agreement on Labor Cooperation" (NAALC), which was a side agreement to the NAFTA, lists 11 labor principles, which include the establishment of minimum employment standards and the payment of minimum wages. Article 3(1) of the NAALC says that although these principles are not intended to "establish

---

[22] International Labor Organization. About the ILO. The ILO is now a specialized agency of the UN, and includes 187 member states.

[23] "Treaty of Versailles." 1919. "Labor Provisions of the Peace Treaties," Article 427, item 3.

[24] See also the list of ILO Conventions.

common minimum standards for their domestic law," each party to the agreement undertakes to "promote compliance with and effectively enforce its labor law through appropriate government action."

The USMCA: Minimum wage levels

When the United States, Mexico, and Canada entered into the USMCA,[25] some of the principles from Annex 1 of the NAALC were amended and moved from the side agreement into the USMCA, and became minimum standards for domestic law. The rules of origin contained in the USMCA require that 40–45 percent of auto content be made by workers earning at least USD $16 per hour. This provision of the USMCA has the effect of establishing corporate behavioral standards, by setting minimum wage levels for some employees of entities that are engaged in the conduct of FDI.

10.5.3 Governmental CSR Standards

The governments of nation-states enact and implement legislated and regulatory standards that govern the business behaviors of individuals and entities that are engaged in the practice of international trade and/or FDI. These standards, which are broadly referred to as *behavioral standards*, can apply to individuals or entities that are nationals of the nation-state that has enacted the standard, and/or to non-national individuals or foreign-funded companies that are engaged in inward FDI to the nation-state that has enacted the standard.[26]

The United States FCPA

The US Foreign Corrupt Practices Act (FCPA) of 1977, established standards of behavior for US individuals and entities engaged in the practice of international trade and/or FDI.

---

[25] The USMCA, which came into effect in July 2020, is discussed in Chapter 9, Section 9.2.1.1.

[26] Some of the terms used in this paragraph are discussed in Chapter 7, Section 7.1.

These standards prohibit the payment (or promise of payment) of bribes—by US nationals and employees, shareholders, directors, and/or agents acting on behalf of a US corporation—to a foreign official, foreign political party or official, or candidate for foreign political office, for the purpose of influencing or inducing an act or decision related to the conduct of international trade or FDI. The FCPA also specifies criminal penalties for corporations and individuals; and distinguishes between prohibited corrupt practices and permitted facilitating payments. The FCPA was amended in 1988, which extended its coverage to persons who should have known or could have known about unlawful payments. It was again amended through the International Anti-Bribery Act of 1998, to implement the provisions of the OECD Anti-Bribery Convention, which came into force in 1999, and extended coverage to non-US nationals operating in the United States.

As discussed in Section 10.4, in some cases the government of a nation-state enacts legislation: (1) to comply with the provisions contained in an intergovernmental agreement that it has ratified (or intends to ratify), and (2) to cause the provisions contained in the agreement to have the force of domestic law.

The US: OECD Anti-Bribery Convention

On November 10, 1998, the United States enacted the International Anti-Bribery Act of 1998, which amended the US Foreign Corrupt Practices Act[27] and provided the implementing legislation for the OECD Anti-Bribery Convention, which the US ratified on December 8, 1998. This action by the US government complied with Article 2 of the OECD Anti-Bribery Convention, which provides that "Each Party shall take such measures as may be necessary, in accordance with its legal principles, to establish the liability of legal persons for the bribery of a foreign public official," and gave the provisions of the convention the force of domestic law.

---

[27] The US Foreign Corrupt Practices Act is discussed in Section 10.5.3.

10.6   The Misuse of Trade-Related Standards

The possible misuse of trade-related standards was anticipated in the first paragraph of Article XX of the GATT, which says that technical barriers to trade must not be used as "a means of arbitrary or unjustifiable discrimination between countries" or as "a disguised restriction on international trade." The misuse of technical barriers to trade, including the misuse of trade-related standards, was the reason that in 1979 some GATT contracting parties, and in 1994 all GATT contracting parties, entered into the "Agreement on Technical Barriers to Trade."

The preamble to the TBT agreement says that "international standards and conformity assessment systems" can facilitate the conduct of international trade. But it also says that "technical regulations and standards, including packaging, marking, and labeling requirements, and procedures for assessment of conformity with technical regulations and standards" can "create unnecessary obstacles to international trade."

Article 2 of the TBT agreement states that: "Members shall ensure that technical regulations are not prepared, adopted, or applied with a view to or with the effect of creating unnecessary obstacles to international trade." The first example in Chapter 3, Section 3.2.4, concerning a government's use of a technical standard to seize electrical tools, appears to have been the misuse of a trade-related standard.

10.7   The Harmonization of Trade-Related Standards

Product, process, services, and corporate behavioral standards are developed and propagated by more than 100 global intergovernmental and non-governmental alliances, associations, councils, consortiums, forums, foundations, groups, institutes, and unions; by more than 20 regional standards organizations; and by hundreds of nationally based standards organizations.

The entity that has done the most to make the standards produced by these numerous organizations consistent or compatible has, since 1946, been and continues to be the ISO. The other organization that is contributing to the harmonization of standards, and especially to the harmonization of trade-related product, process, and services standards, is the

WTO—through its TBT agreement, the GATS, and related committees, which have established norms for standard-setting organizations.

Article 2.4 of the TBT agreement provides that governments use international standards "as a basis for their technical regulations"; Article 2.6 states that "With a view to harmonizing technical regulations on as wide a basis as possible, Members shall play a full part ... in the preparation by appropriate international standardizing bodies of international standards for products for which they either have adopted, or expect to adopt, technical regulations"; Article 5.4 provides that governments use international standards "as a basis for their conformity assessment procedures"; Article 5.5 states that "With a view to harmonizing conformity assessment procedures on as wide a basis as possible, Members shall play a full part ... in the preparation by appropriate international standardizing bodies of guides and recommendations for conformity assessment procedures"; Article 11.2 provides for technical assistance on the establishment of National standardizing bodies, and participation in international standardizing bodies; and Article 12.5 states that WTO Members "shall take such reasonable measures as may be available to them to ensure that international standardizing bodies and international systems for conformity assessment are organized and operated in a way which facilitates active and representative participation of relevant bodies in all Members."

Annex 3 of the TBT agreement provides a *Code of Good Practice for the Preparation, Adoption and Application of Standards* (TBT Code), which has been accepted by 138 standardizing bodies, in 94 countries. Part E of the TBT Code states that "standards shall not be prepared, adopted or applied with the view to, or with the effect of, creating unnecessary obstacles to international trade"; and Part G provides that, with a view to harmonizing standards on as wide a basis as possible, a standardizing body shall play a full part in the preparation "of international standards regarding subject matter for which it either has adopted, or expects to adopt, standards."

Article VII:5 of the GATS provides that: "Members shall work in cooperation with relevant intergovernmental and non-governmental organizations towards the establishment and adoption of common international standards and criteria for recognition and common international standards for the practice of relevant services trades and professions."

CHAPTER 11

The Harmonization of Laws

Contents

11.1 Introduction

When an individual or entity is engaged in the practice of international trade and/or FDI, they are operating in more than one nation-state and in more than one legal jurisdiction, and are subject to more than one set of legal principles and laws.

Also, the conduct of international trade and/or FDI includes the use of contracts that are entered into in different jurisdictions, that are between parties from different jurisdictions, and that govern the commercial operations of entities in different jurisdictions.

11.2 The Conflict of Laws

The issue of legal jurisdiction can be problematic for entities engaged in the practice of international trade and/or FDI, because entities engaged in international trade must comply simultaneously with the laws of exporting and importing countries, and entities engaged in FDI must comply simultaneously with the laws of their home country and the laws of their host country or countries. These conditions are compounded and made more complex when an entity has entered into multiple international contracts covered by multiple jurisdictions, operates in multiple countries and multiple legal systems, and is subject to multiple sets of legal principles and multiple sets of laws.

Each of these conditions can be more problematic when there are differences in the laws in different jurisdictions. Differences in the laws of different jurisdictions that affect individuals and entities are referred to as the *conflict of laws*.

11.2.1   In Domestic Law

In domestic law, the conflict of laws occurs within countries that use a federal system, because these countries (which include Australia, Canada, and the US) have multiple jurisdictions. The legal systems in each of these countries include provisions for resolving domestic conflicts of laws, which can include providing the highest court in the country's judicial system (such as the High Court of Australia, the Supreme Court of Canada, or the Supreme Court of the United States) with the authority to decide jurisdictional issues.

11.2.2   In International Law

In international law, the term *conflict of laws* refers to the differences in the laws of different jurisdictions, to the procedural rules that govern the use of laws from different jurisdictions, to how courts determine which of these laws apply to a specific dispute, and to the efforts by nation-states and intergovernmental organizations to reduce the adverse effects of conflicting laws. The term is also used when referring to the body of conventions, model laws, legal guidelines, and other agreements between nation-states that are designed to reduce or to bridge differences in the laws of individual nation-states—which affect the international activities of individuals and entities.

The *conflict of laws* can also be seen as a process for harmonizing the laws of separate nation-states, and for developing a consensus among nationstates relating to laws that affect the international activities of individuals and entities.

11.2.3 Private International Law

The body of international law that governs the relationships between nation-states is referred to as *public international law*. To differentiate *public international law* from the differences in the laws that affect the international activities of individuals and entities, the *conflict of laws* is also called *private international law*.

The usage of the terms *conflict of laws* and *private international law* varies by country. For example, the term *conflict of laws* is used more in Australia, Canada, the UK, and the US; the term *private international law* is used more in continental European countries, and in countries in Africa and Latin America.

11.2.3.1 Choice of Laws

Because the conflict of laws instruments that are discussed in Section 11.3 are intended to establish which law applies in a particular situation, the conflict of laws is also referred to as the *choice of laws*.

11.2.3.2 Harmonization of Laws

Because the conflict of laws refers to the efforts by nation-states and inter-governmental organizations to reduce the adverse effects of conflicting laws, it is also referred to as the *harmonization of laws*.

The term *harmonization* is sometimes used in the area of public international law. For example, the word *harmonization* is used in the text of the "Agreement on Rules of Origin," and in the title and text of the "International Convention on the Simplification and Harmonization of Customs Procedures."[1] The term *harmonization of laws*, however,

---

[1] These instruments are discussed in Chapter 2, Section 2.4.2.

is a synonym for the terms *conflict of laws*, *choice of laws*, and *private international law*.

11.3   Instruments and Mechanisms for the Harmonization of Laws

The harmonization of laws is effected through the work of intergovernmental organizations, and through intergovernmental instruments that have been entered into by nation-states.

11.3.1   Private International Law Instruments

Instruments for the harmonization of laws include:

1. United Nations Convention on Contracts for the International Sale of Goods
2. Convention on the Recognition and Enforcement of Foreign Arbitral Awards
3. Convention on Stolen or Illegally Exported Cultural Objects
4. Convention on International Interests in Mobile Equipment
5. Convention on the Service Abroad of Judicial and Extrajudicial Documents in Civil or Commercial Matters
6. Convention on the Taking of Evidence Abroad in Civil or Commercial Matters

11.3.2   Private International Law Mechanisms

There are several intergovernmental organizations that focus solely on, or whose work includes, the harmonization of laws.

11.3.2.1   UNCITRAL

The United Nations Commission on International Trade Law (UNCITRAL) was established by the General Assembly of the United Nations in 1966, "to promote the progressive harmonization and unification of international trade law." UNCITRAL, which is located in Vienna, has developed more than 40 intergovernmental instruments in the field of international trade law and commercial law reform. The first two instruments on the list in Section 11.3.1 were created under the auspice of UNCITRAL.

11.3.2.2   UNIDROIT

The International Institute for the Unification of Private Law (UNIDROIT) was created in 1926 as an organ of the League of Nations. UNIDROIT, which is located in Rome, is now an autonomous intergovernmental organization for "modernizing, harmonizing and coordinating private and in particular commercial law." Instruments 3 and 4 on the list in Section 11.3.1 were created under the auspice of UNIDROIT.

11.3.2.3   HCCH

The first Hague Conference on Private International Law (HCCH) was held in 1893; in 1955, it became a permanent intergovernmental organization. HCCH develops and services multilateral legal instruments for the purpose of achieving the "progressive unification" of private international law relating to "personal, family, and commercial situations." Instruments 5 and 6 on the list in Section 11.3.1 were created under the auspice of the HCCH.

11.3.3   The US and the Harmonization of Laws

The United States became a member of UNCITRAL in 1966, of UNIDROIT in 1964, and of HCCH in 1964. The US has ratified all the instruments listed in Section 11.3.1.

CHAPTER 12

The Settlement of Disputes

Contents

12.1 Primary Classifications

International disputes can be classified by: (1) the subject of the dispute, (2) the identity of the parties to the dispute, and (3) the law or laws that are applicable to the dispute.

12.1.1 The Subject of the Dispute

In the field of international relations, the subject of a dispute can be classified as political, security-related, or commercial. Other subject classifications include territory, ideology, religion, and human rights. These subject classifications are in some cases seen as subcategories of political or security-related disputes. Also, some international disputes defy single-category classification, because they are covered by two or more subject categories.

International commercial disputes can be classified as either trade disputes or investment disputes. The term *investment disputes* refers to disputes related to FDI.

12.1.2 The Parties to the Dispute

The parties to international commercial disputes are divided into two categories: *nationstates*, and *nationals of nation-states*.[1] For example: Japan is a nation-state; Toyota is a national of a nation-state. The term *nationals of nation-states* include individuals, corporations, and other entities. The division between nationstates and nationals of nation-states results in three types of international commercial disputes:

1. Disputes between nation-states;
2. Disputes between nationals of different nation-states; and
3. Disputes between nation-states and nationals of other nation-states.

12.1.2.1 Disputes Between Nation-States

The dispute between Brazil and the United States over subsidies the US government pays to US cotton farmers is a dispute between nation-states.[2]

---

[1] As discussed in Chapter 7, Section 7.1.3, references to nation-states and nationals of nation-states include separate customs territories, and nationals or residents of separate customs territories.

[2] This dispute is discussed in Chapter 4, Section 4.3.4.3.

12.1.2.2   Disputes Between Nationals of Different Nation-States

DVD manufacturers in China and non-Chinese owners of DVD technology

From 2000 through 2006, Chinese companies that manufacture DVD players were engaged in a dispute with Japanese, European, and US companies that own DVD technology (including Hitachi, Panasonic, Mitsubishi, Toshiba, JVC, Philips, Sony, and Pioneer) over the payment of royalties. This was a dispute between nationals of different nation-states.

12.1.2.3   Disputes Between Nation-States and Nationals of Other Nation-States

The EU and DVD manufacturers in China

The dispute over royalty payments for the use of DVD technology led the European Union to block the importation of Chinese-made DVD players. This resulted in a dispute between the European Union and the Chinese companies that manufacture DVD players.

Because the EU is a separate customs territory, this dispute is seen as being between a nation-state (the EU) and nationals of another nation-state (the Chinese manufacturers of DVD players).

12.1.3   Applicable Law

Article 1, paragraph 1, of the UN Charter says the settlement of international disputes should be:

" … in conformity with the principles of justice and international law …" The type of applicable law can be determined by the identity of the parties to the dispute, by the subject of the dispute, and/or by the location of the dispute.

12.1.3.1   Nation-States

If the parties to a dispute are nationstates, the applicable law may be customary international law or treaty law. The sources of *customary international law* used by the International Court of Justice include "international custom, as evidence of a general practice accepted as law, ... general principles of law recognized by civilized nations, ... judicial decisions," and the teachings of eminent legal scholars.[3] Customary international law can also include treaty law that over time has become "international custom, as evidence of a general practice accepted as law." Because the sources of customary international law include the body of precedent established in judicial decisions, it is similar to domestic common law.

> RCEP Agreement
>
> Annex 10A of the RCEP Agreement[4] says: "The parties confirm their shared understanding that 'customary international law' ... results from a general and consistent practice of States that they follow from a sense of legal obligation."

The term *treaty law* refers to law that comes from provisions that are contained in international instruments, which are written agreements.[5] Because the source of treaty law is written agreements, it is sometimes called *black letter law*. Because the source of treaty law is specific citable instruments, international treaty law is similar to domestic statute law.

> Japan and Ukraine: Safeguards
>
> In 2013, Japan brought a complaint to the WTO Dispute Settlement Body against Ukraine "regarding the definitive safeguard measures[6] imposed by Ukraine on imports of certain

---

[3] ICJ Statute, Article 38(1).

[4] The RCEP Agreement is discussed in Chapter 7, Section 7.3.2.1.

[5] This characteristic of international instruments is discussed in Chapter 7, Section 7.3.

[6] Safeguards are discussed in Chapter 3, Section 3.3.3.

passenger cars and the investigation that led to the imposition of those measures."[7] In this complaint, Japan claimed the measures taken by Ukraine were "inconsistent with Articles 2.1, 3.1, 4.1(a), 4.1(b), 4.2(a), 4.2(b), 4.2(c), 5.1, 7.1, 7.4, 8.1, 12.1(a), 12.1, 12.2, and 12.3 of the "Agreement on Safeguards"; and with Articles II:1(b) and XIX:1(a) of the GATT 1994." Japan's action was based on specific provisions of agreements to which Japan and Ukraine are parties, and was, therefore, a use of treaty law—or black letter law.

12.1.3.2   Nationals of Different Nation-States

If the parties to a dispute are companies that are nationals of different nation-states, the applicable law is the laws of the nation-state in which the disputed action has occurred—unless there is a prior written agreement between the parties to use an extra-national alternative.[8]

12.1.3.3   Nation-States and Nationals of Other Nation-States

If the parties to a dispute are the government of a nation-state and a commercial entity that is a national of another state, the dispute is governed by the laws of the nation-state in which the disputed action has occurred—unless there is a prior written agreement between the parties that provides for the use of an extra-national alternative. These extra-national alternatives are discussed in Section 12.2.5.

12.1.3.4   The Conflict of Laws

In some international commercial disputes, the applicable law can include laws of the company's host-country and home-country.[9] If there

---

[7] Press release, Dispute Settlement Japan–Ukraine.

[8] The prefix *extra* in the term *extra-national* means "outside of." The use of extra-national alternatives is discussed in Section 12.2.4. As discussed in Section 12.2.4.3, the use of extra-national alternatives can be subject to restrictions.

[9] The terms *home country* and *host country* are discussed in Chapter 7, Section 7.1.2.1.

are differences in applicable home-country and host-country laws, this can result in the conflict of laws.[10]

12.2 Dispute Settlement Mechanisms

The term *dispute settlement mechanism* (DSM) refers to any mechanism that can be used to facilitate the resolution of a dispute. DSMs can be either organizational or functional mechanisms.[11]

12.2.1 The Need for International DSMs

The processes and mechanisms used in the settlement of domestic commercial disputes are, in most cases, unsuitable for the settlement of international commercial disputes.[12]

12.2.1.1 For National Governments

Commercial disputes between nation-states cannot be settled using the courts of either nation-state that is a party to a dispute, because the legal playing field would not be level.

> Brazil and the US: Subsidies
> The dispute between Brazil and the US, over subsidies the US government pays to US cotton farmers, cannot be settled using the courts of Brazil or the United States.

12.2.1.2 For Commercial Entities

The legal dictum *locus regit actum* says, inter alia, that disputes should be decided using the courts of the location where the disputed action

---

[10] The conflict of laws is discussed in Chapter 11, Section 11.2.
[11] Organizational and functional mechanisms are discussed in Chapter 7, Sections 7.4.2 and 7.4.3.
[12] The exception to this generalization is the use of third-country courts, which is discussed in Section 12.4.1.

has occurred.[13] But for entities engaged in the practice of international trade and/or FDI, the use of a host-country's courts can be problematic, because the legal playing field may not be level:

1. *Nationals of different nation-states.* In disputes between nationals of different nation-states, there can be a problem using the courts of the country where the dispute has occurred—if one party to the dispute is a foreign national[14] and the other party is a national of the host-country. In these cases, the legal playing field may not be level because the host-country national may receive preferential treatment by the host country's courts.
2. *Nation-states and nationals of other nation-states.* In disputes between nation-states and nationals of other nation-states, the legal playing field may not be level because the host-country government may receive preferential treatment by the host country's courts.

12.2.2   The Classification of International DSMs

DSMs are classified using several criteria, which include: (1) the parties that are permitted to use the DSM; (2) the organization within which the DSM is located, or with which the DSM is affiliated; (3) the subject areas covered by the DSM; (4) the types of law applied by the DSM; (5) the DSM's geographical scope; and (6) the dispute settlement procedures offered by the DSM. Dispute settlement procedures are discussed in Section 12.3. The dispute settlement procedures offered by the WTO Dispute Settlement Body and other DSMs are discussed in Sections 12.4 and 12.5.

DSMs that are used to facilitate the resolution of international trade and foreign investment disputes can, like types of disputes, be grouped into three categories:

1. DSMs for the settlement of disputes between nation-states
2. DSMs for the settlement of disputes between nationals of different nation-states

---

[13] *Locus regit actum* is discussed in Chapter 6, Section 6.5.2.1
[14] The term *foreign national* is discussed in Chapter 7, Section 7.1.2.1.

3. DSMs for the settlement of disputes between nation-states and nationals of other nation-states

Most DSMs for the settlement of international commercial disputes are operational sub-units of global or regional intergovernmental organizations. In some cases, they are functional mechanisms of those intergovernmental organizations.

12.2.3   DSMs for Disputes Between Nation-States

DSMs that are used to settle international commercial disputes between nation-states can be classified as trade related or not trade related, and as global or regional.

12.2.3.1   Global DSMs for Disputes Between Nation-States

The principal global DSM for the settlement of trade-related disputes between nation-states is the WTO Dispute Settlement Body (DSB), which is discussed in Section 12.4. Economic and commercial disputes that are not related to trade can be decided by the International Court of Justice or by a subject-specific DSM.

Offshore oil and gas reserves
Some nation-states have used the ICJ to settle disputes over offshore oil and gas reserves. Other nation-states have taken these disputes to the International Tribunal for the Law of the Sea, which was created by the "United Nations Convention on the Law of the Sea" (UNCLOS).

12.2.3.2   Regional DSMs for Disputes Between Nation-States

Some of the regional trade blocs have established functional or organizational mechanisms for settling disputes between their member states:

- The ASEAN Free Trade Area's DSM was established by the ASEAN "Protocol on Enhanced Dispute Settlement Mechanism" of 1996 and 2004.

- The Economic Community of West African States (ECOWAS) used a 1993 treaty revision to establish a Court of Justice for resolving disputes between its member states.[15]
- The MERCOSUR Common Market Group[16] and the USMCA have DSMs for settling commercial disputes.
- The AfCFTA Agreement includes a "Protocol on Rules and Procedures on the Settlement of Disputes," which provides for the establishment of an AfCFTA Dispute Settlement Body.
- The RCEP Dispute Settlement procedures are contained in Chapter 19 of the RCEP Agreement.

The development and use of regional DSMs is supported by the UN Charter. The list of procedures contained in Article 33 of the Charter includes the use of "regional agencies or arrangements."[17]

12.2.4   DSMs for Disputes Between Nationals of Different Nation-States

Disputes between commercial entities that are nationals of different nation-states must be settled using the courts of the nation-state in which the dispute occurs—unless the contractual agreement between the parties to the dispute provides for the use of an extra-national dispute settlement mechanism. There are two types of extra-national alternatives: third-country options and institutional options.

12.2.4.1   Third-Country Options

Some agreements between commercial entities that are nationals of different nation-states provide that, in the case of a dispute, the parties will use the courts of a third country.

---

[15] ECOWAS has 15 member countries.
[16] MERCOSUR member countries are Argentina, Brazil, Paraguay, and Uruguay.
[17] The procedures listed in Article 33 of the UN Charter are discussed in Section 12.3.1.

China, the US, and Sweden: Pepsi

The agreement between PepsiCo (a US company) and its Chinese equity joint venture (EJV) partner in Chengdu, Sichuan Province, designated the Court of Commercial Arbitration in Stockholm as the forum for the settlement of disputes. In this example, Sweden is a third country, because it is neither China nor the United States.

In some cases, the third-country option employs the courts of one third country, and the laws of another third country.

12.2.4.2   Institutional Options

Some contractual agreements between commercial entities that are nationals of different nation-states provide that, in the case of a dispute, the parties will use a specific international DSM that has been established for the purpose of settling disputes between nationals of different nation-states. These DSMs include:

- International Court of Arbitration,[18] which is the dispute-settlement body of the International Chamber of Commerce (ICC);
- Arbitration and Mediation Center of the World Intellectual Property Organization.[19]

12.2.4.3   The Exhaustion of Local Remedies

Some nation-states require that commercial entities that are parties to a dispute must use the full range of procedures offered by their country's courts before taking a dispute to an extra-national dispute settlement mechanism. This requirement is called the *exhaustion of local remedies*.[20]

---

[18] The International Court of Arbitration is located in Paris.
[19] The WIPO and its DSM are located in Geneva.
[20] The exhaustion of local remedies is discussed in Chapter 6, Section 6.5.2.1.

Even where a nation-state does not require the exhaustion of local remedies, in some cases a dispute between commercial entities can only be taken to an extra-national DSM if this has first been approved by local courts.

China, the US, and Sweden: Pepsi

In 2003, PepsiCo brought a legal action against its Chinese equity joint venture partner in Chengdu, Sichuan Province, over mismanagement, financial irregularities, and control. This dispute was first submitted to Chengdu courts, which: (1) approved the dispute-settlement clause contained in the EJV agreement, and (2) approved that the dispute be decided by the Court of Commercial Arbitration in Stockholm.

12.2.5   DSMs for Disputes Between Nation-States and Nationals of Other Nation-States

Disputes between nation-states and nationals of other nation-states must be settled using the courts of the nation-state in which the dispute occurs—unless the FDI agreement between the company and the host-country government includes a compromissory clause that provides for the use of an extra-national dispute settlement mechanism, or unless this provision is included in a governing bilateral or multilateral agreement.

12.2.5.1   ISDS

Since the 1960s, an increasing number of bilateral and multilateral trade and investment agreements have included extra-national procedures for the settlement of disputes between nation-states and nationals of other nation-states. The dispute-settlement articles of these agreements are referred to generically as *Investor-State Dispute Settlement* (ISDS) clauses.

The Office of the US Trade Representative (USTR) says that "Various forms of ISDS are now a part of over 3,000 agreements worldwide, of which the United States is party to 50."[21]

---

[21] USTR, ISDS.

12.2.5.2   ICSID

The most widely used mechanism for the settlement of disputes between nation-states and nationals of other nation-states is the International Center for the Settlement of Investment Disputes (ICSID).[22] ICSID was created by the World Bank in 1966,[23] through the "Convention on the Settlement of Investment Disputes between States and Nationals of Other States." The ICSID Convention has been signed and ratified by more than 150 states.[24] ICSID has administered more than 840 cases.

12.2.5.3   Third-Country Options

Foreign-funded companies and the governments of host-countries have also chosen to use third-country options.[25]

> Peru and Japan: Swedish courts
> The compromissory clause in an agreement between a Japanese oil pipeline construction company and the government of Peru provided that, in the case of a dispute, the parties would use Swedish courts and UK law.

12.3   Dispute Settlement Procedures

The term *dispute settlement procedures* refers to the methods used to settle disputes. International dispute settlement procedures are characterized by: (1) the availability of a large number of different procedures, and (2) the diversity of these procedures.

---

[22] ICSID is located in Washington, D.C.
[23] The World Bank is discussed in Chapter 8, Section 8.2.2.2.
[24] The United States signed the ICSID Convention in 1965, and deposited its instrument of ratification in 1966.
[25] Third-country options are discussed in Section 12.2.4.1.

12.3.1   The Underlying Principle

Article 33 of the UN Charter[26] says:

> The parties to any dispute, the continuance of which is likely to endanger the maintenance of international peace and security, shall, first of all, seek a solution by negotiation, enquiry, mediation, conciliation, arbitration, judicial settlement, resort to regional agencies or arrangements, or other peaceful means of their own choice.

Article 33 of the charter, and especially the phrase "shall, first of all, seek a solution," is seen as containing the principle that parties to a dispute should seek a solution at the lowest adversarial level. The procedures listed in Article 33 are arranged in approximate hierarchical order—from procedures that are less adversarial to procedures that are more adversarial. An exact hierarchical ordering would be: enquiry, negotiation, conciliation, mediation, arbitration, and judicial settlement.

Although Article 33 refers to disputes related to "international peace and security," the practice of using the least adversarial procedure has come to influence all areas of international dispute settlement, including the settlement of commercial disputes. Also, although Article 33 addresses the settlement of disputes between nation-states, the principle contained in this article is applied by many of the DSMs that are used by commercial entities that are engaged in the practice of international trade and/or FDI.

12.3.2   The Six-Procedure Hierarchy

The procedures used to settle international disputes, including international commercial disputes, can be arranged in a six-element hierarchy, which is derived from Article 33 of the UN Charter, and which begins with the procedure that is least adversarial—followed by procedures that are increasingly more adversarial:

1. Negotiation/Consultation
2. Good offices

---

[26] Article 33 is contained in Chapter VI: Pacific Settlement of Disputes.

3. Conciliation
4. Mediation
5. Arbitration
6. Adjudication/Litigation

12.3.2.1 Negotiation/Consultation

The primary characteristics of negotiation/consultation are that the procedure (1) is non-binding, and (2) does not involve the participation of a third party. This procedure does not result in a legal conclusion, but is intended to facilitate the reaching of a mutually acceptable solution. The terms *negotiation* and *consultation* are often used interchangeably. There has, however, been an increase in the use of the term *consultation* (rather than *negotiation*), which may be because consultation is the first step in the WTO dispute settlement system.[27]

12.3.2.2 Good Offices

The good offices procedure is similar to negotiation/consultation, but includes the participation of a third party. An important characteristic of good offices, however, is that the participation of the third party is limited to facilitating the meeting of the parties to the dispute—and does not include the third party's participation in the negotiations/consultations.

12.3.2.3 Conciliation

The conciliation procedure is similar to good offices, but the conciliator participates in the negotiation/consultation process. The role of the conciliator, however, is limited—and the conciliator is not positioned between the parties to the dispute. In the conciliation procedure, the two parties are still discussing the situation directly, and the role of the conciliator is to facilitate the process.

---

[27] Consultation in the WTO DSB system is discussed in Sections 12.4.3, 12.4.3.1, and 12.4.4.

12.3.2.4   Mediation

Mediation is similar to conciliation, but the mediator is positioned between the parties to the dispute. Also, in mediation, the mediator may propose a solution to the parties.

12.3.2.5   Arbitration

Arbitration also uses the participation of a third party, called the *arbitrator*. In arbitration: (1) the parties to the dispute do not engage in negotiation/consultation, but present their arguments to the arbitrator; (2) the procedure results in a legal conclusion; and (3) the legal conclusion is binding. Arbitration is not, however, a judicial procedure: It does not take place in a court of law and is not subject to legal structures and requirements. Because of this, an arbitrator has more flexibility than a judge when deciding how a procedure is handled, how a decision is reached, and the terms and scope of the decision.

12.3.2.6   Adjudication/Litigation

Adjudication, which is also called *litigation*, shares some similarities with arbitration: it results in a legal conclusion, and the decision of the judge (or judges) is binding upon the parties to the dispute. The difference, however, is that adjudication/litigation is a judicial procedure. It takes place in a court of law and is subject to strict legal structures and requirements.

12.4   The WTO Dispute Settlement Body

The WTO Dispute Settlement Body was created by the 1994 Uruguay Round Understanding on Rules and Procedures Governing the Settlement of Disputes, which is commonly called the *Dispute Settlement Understanding*, as the 1994 Understanding,[28] or simply as the Understanding.

---

[28] The term *1994 Understanding* is used to differentiate this instrument from the 1979 Understanding Regarding Notification, Consultation, Dispute Settlement, and Surveillance.

All members of the WTO are members of the Dispute Settlement Body.[29] Any reference to the DSB means, therefore, all members of the WTO. Article 1, paragraph 1, of the 1994 Understanding says its rules and procedures shall apply to consultations and the settlement of disputes between WTO Members. The DSB can, however, also be used by countries and by separate customs territories that are not WTO members—if both parties to the dispute agree to use the DSB mechanism.

12.4.1 Applicable Law

Article 1, paragraph 1, says the 1994 Understanding applies to "disputes brought pursuant to the consultation and dispute settlement provisions of the agreements listed in Appendix 1." Because DSB disputes are based on provisions contained in instruments, the DSB uses treaty law.[30] Articles 3 and 27 of the 1994 Understanding refer to "provisions of ... agreements in accordance with customary rules of interpretation of public international law"[31] and "historical ... aspects of the matters dealt with"—which indicate the DSB's decisions may also apply or be influenced by customary international law.[32]

12.4.2 Functional Mechanisms

The WTO DSB is characterized by a unique dispute settlement system, which has three functional mechanisms: (1) panels, (2) the Appellate Body (AB), and (3) the DSB. This system was developed by the de facto GATT organization and the GATT Secretariat between 1948 and 1994. The system was codified and modified during the Tokyo Round (1973–1979) and Uruguay Round (1986–1994) of multilateral trade negotiations,[33] and, most significantly, by the provisions contained in the 1994 Understanding.

---

[29] This is discussed in Chapter 8, Section 8.5.1.1.

[30] The term *treaty law* is discussed in Section 12.1.3.1.

[31] The term *public international law* is discussed in Chapter 11, Section 11.2.3.

[32] The term *customary international law* is discussed in Section 12.1.3.1.

[33] The Tokyo Round and Uruguay Round of multilateral trade negotiations are discussed in Chapter 8, Sections 8.4.3.1 through 8.4.3.3.

12.4.2.1   Panels

In 1952, the GATT began to use panels to investigate complaints by contracting parties. The term *panel* was used to emphasize the technical objectivity of the persons engaged in these investigations. The panels, their composition, and their terms of operation have been subject to many changes[34]—and have evolved into the panel procedure that is detailed in Articles 6 through 16 of the 1994 Understanding.

Article 6 of the 1994 Understanding says that, at the request of a "complaining party,"[35] the Secretariat of the DSB will establish an ad hoc panel (composed of three persons) to make an objective assessment of the dispute and to report findings and conclusions to the DSB.

Article 15 of the 1994 Understanding, Interim Review Stage, allows for the parties to a dispute to make comments on a panel report, following which "the final panel report" will be circulated to Members.

Article 16, paragraph 4, Adoption of Panel reports, says that following the circulation of a report, and absent an appeal by a party to the dispute, the panel report will be adopted by the DSB—unless the DSB decides by consensus not to adopt the report. This adoption provision, which is referred to as *reverse consensus*, was an innovation. It replaced the consensus requirement used by the de facto GATT organization, which required that, for a panel report to be adopted, it had to receive the affirming votes of all contracting parties—which meant adoption could be vetoed by a single negative vote (or, some would argue, even by an absence or an abstention). The *reverse consensus* rule means that a panel report is adopted unless there is a consensus of dissenting votes—that is, unless every member votes against it. This change reduced dramatically the possibility that a panel report would not be approved.

12.4.2.2   The Appellate Body

Article 17, paragraph 1, of the 1994 Understanding, provides for the establishment of "a standing Appellate Body" that "shall hear appeals

---

[34] Hudec. n.d. "WTO Dispute Settlement Procedure."
[35] The term *complaining party* refers to a WTO Member that is bringing a complaint against another WTO Member.

from panel cases." The addition of the Appellate Body, and the provisions governing its structure and operation, were considered to be one of the most important achievements of the Uruguay Round of multilateral trade negotiations;[36] to be one of the most important provisions of the 1994 Understanding; and to be one of the most significant distinctions between the de facto GATT organization and the WTO.

Article 17, paragraph 4, provides that "only parties to the dispute … may appeal a panel report," but third parties may make written submissions to, and be given an opportunity to be heard by, the AB. Paragraph 6, says "an appeal shall be limited to issues of law covered in the panel report and legal interpretations developed by the panel." Paragraph 13 says, the AB "may uphold, modify, or reverse the legal findings and conclusions of the panel."

The rules governing the adoption of Appellate Body reports include the same *reverse consensus* innovation that applies to the adoption of panel reports. Article 17, paragraph 14, of the 1994 Understanding says: "An Appellate Body report shall be adopted by the DSB and unconditionally accepted by the parties to the dispute unless the DSB decides by consensus not to adopt the Appellate Body report."

12.4.2.3   The Appointment of AB Members

Article 17, paragraphs 1 and 2, of the 1994 Understanding provide that the Appellate Body be composed of seven persons, each of whom is appointed to a fouryear term, and "three of whom shall serve on any one case." By tradition, the United States, the EU, and Japan have each had an AB member. Also, by tradition, any AB member who has been willing to serve a second term was reappointed automatically.

Beginning in 2011, the government of the United States started to block the reappointment or appointment of Appellate Body members. By mid-2017, these actions by the United States had resulted in the AB having only three members (which is the number required to serve on a case), and by December 2019, the number of AB members was reduced to one—which meant the AB was no longer able to function.

---

[36] The Uruguay Round is discussed in Chapter 8, Section 8.4.3.2.

A 2021 report on the Appellate Body, by the US Congressional Research Service, cites the United States Trade Representative as saying that the reason the US government withheld approval of AB member appointments was because the AB had "exceeded its mandate, as established by the WTO rules, by (1) disregarding the deadline for issuing decisions; (2) allowing former members to decide cases; (3) reviewing panel findings of fact; (4) issuing advisory opinions; (5) treating prior decisions as binding precedent; (6) declining to make recommendations about the WTO-compatibility of measures that expire after panel establishment; and (7) encroaching on other WTO bodies."[37]

12.4.3   Procedures Offered by the DSB

The dispute settlement procedures offered by the WTO DSB are consultation, good offices, conciliation, mediation, arbitration, and the panels and Appellate Review system.

12.4.3.1   Consultation

Article 3, General Provisions, of the 1994 Understanding says that WTO Members "affirm their adherence" to the principles, rules, and procedures for the management of disputes contained in Articles XXII and XXIII of the GATT. Article XXII, Consultation, of the GATT, provides for consultation between the contracting parties "with respect to any matter affecting the operation of this Agreement."

Article 4, Consultations, of the 1994 Understanding repeats the "consultation" language from the GATT, and provides extensive details concerning the use of the consultation procedure. These details cover notifying the DSB of the initiation and status of consultations, the confidentiality of consultations, and the times allowed for responding to a request for consultation.

12.4.3.2   Good Offices, Conciliation, and Mediation

Article 5 of the 1994 Understanding says that "good offices, conciliation, or mediation may be requested at any time by any party to a dispute"

---

[37] Congressional Research Service. 2021. *The WTO Appellate Body.*

and that "if the parties to a dispute agree, procedures for good offices, conciliation or mediation may continue while the panel process proceeds."

12.4.3.3   Arbitration

Article 25 of the 1994 Understanding offers "expeditious arbitration within the WTO as an alternative means of dispute settlement" if both parties to a dispute agree to use this procedure, and if the parties "agree to abide by the arbitration award."

12.4.3.4   Panels and the Appellate Body procedures

The 1994 Understanding does not address directly the procedures used by panels and the Appellate Body. But Article 12, Paragraphs 6 and 7, say the parties must submit their arguments to the panel, which then reports its findings and recommendations to the DSB.

Articles 16 and 17 discuss the adoption of panel and Appellate Body reports. These articles of the 1994 Understanding indicate that the procedures used by the DSB panels and Appellate Review system are a form of arbitration,[38] except that, in each case, the role of arbitrator is divided between the panel and the DSB and, if there is an appeal, the Appellate Body.

Article 21 of the 1994 Understanding includes measures for the prompt and effective implementation of and compliance with the DSB's recommendations and/or rulings.

12.4.4   Characteristics of the DSB System

There are three characteristics that distinguish the DSB system: its range of dispute settlement alternatives; its panels and Appellate Review system; and its emphasis on consultation. The GATT and the 1994 Understanding designate consultation as the first step to be taken by a WTO member that has a complaint against another member.

---

[38] Arbitration is discussed in Section 12.3.2.5.

Japan and Ukraine: Safeguards

In October 2013, when Japan initiated its complaint against Ukraine relating to the use of safeguard measures,[39] it requested consultations with Ukraine. In November 2013, the European Union and Russia requested that they be allowed to join these consultations, and Ukraine informed the DSB it had accepted the requests by the EU and Russia.

Russia and the EU: Anti-dumping

In 2014, Russia issued "a request for consultations with the European Union regarding anti-dumping measures imposed by the European Union on several products imported from Russia, including ammonium nitrate and steel products,"[40] and notified the WTO Secretariat of this request.[41]

Because consultation has the lowest adversarial level of any of the procedures discussed in Section 12.4.3, this provision of the GATT and the DSB is consistent with the principle contained in Article 33 of the UN Charter—of seeking a solution at the lowest adversarial level.[42] Due to this emphasis on the use of consultation, more than half of the disputes brought to the DSB have been resolved without reaching the panel level.

12.4.5   The Purpose of DSB Procedures

The purpose of the procedures offered by the DSB is not to penalize a member for not complying with the WTO's rules or requirements—or to compensate the complainant. Rather, the purpose is to resolve the dispute by finding a mutually acceptable solution; or, at least, to remove the cause of the dispute. The 1994 Understanding says:

The aim of the dispute settlement mechanism is to secure a positive solution to a dispute. A solution mutually acceptable to the

---

[39] This complaint is discussed in Section 12.1.3.1.
[40] Press release, Dispute Settlement Russia–EU.
[41] This was the first dispute originated by Russia with the WTO DSB.
[42] This principle is discussed in Section 12.3.1.

parties to a dispute and consistent with the covered agreements is clearly to be preferred.[43]

In the absence of a mutually agreed solution, the first objective of the dispute settlement mechanism is usually to secure the withdrawal of the measures concerned if these are found to be inconsistent with the provisions of any of the covered agreements.

Where a panel or the Appellate Body concludes that a measure is inconsistent with a covered agreement, it shall recommend that the Member concerned bring the measure into conformity with that agreement.[44]

In addition to its recommendations, the panel or Appellate Body may suggest ways in which the Member concerned could implement the recommendations.

12.5   Procedures Offered by Other DSMs

In the areas of international trade and FDI, most dispute settlement mechanisms support the principle of seeking a solution at the lowest adversarial level by offering at least two procedures:

- The Arbitration and Mediation Center of the WIPO offers mediation and arbitration procedures.
- ICSID offers conciliation and arbitration.
- Article 23 of the "ASEAN Charter" says that "parties to the dispute may request the Chairman of ASEAN or the Secretary-General of ASEAN, acting in an ex-officio capacity, to provide good offices, conciliation or mediation."
- The WTO Dispute Settlement Body offers five dispute settlement procedures, which are discussed in Section 12.4.3, and requires that consultation be the first step in resolving a dispute when using the DSB.
- The USMCA Dispute Settlement provisions, which are contained in Chapter 31 of the agreement, allow for the use

---

[43] 1994 Understanding, Article 3, General Provisions, Paragraph 7.
[44] 1994 Understanding, Article 19, Panel and Appellate Body Recommendations.

of consultations, good offices, conciliation, mediation, and a dispute settlement panel.

- The AfCFTA Dispute Settlement Body procedures, which are contained in Articles 7 through 24 of the AfCFTA Agreement, Protocol on Rules and Procedures on the Settlement of Disputes, are: consultation, good offices, conciliation, mediation, the use of panels, and appeals. Article 20 provides for "A standing Appellate Body."
- The RCEP Dispute Settlement procedures, which are contained in Chapter 19 of the RCEP Agreement, are: consultation, good offices, conciliation, mediation, and the use of panels.

The last three DSMs on this list offer the same five procedures as the WTO DSB: consultations, good offices, conciliation, mediation, and a dispute settlement panel; the consultation procedure is presented first; and the procedures are presented in ascending adversarial order. But, unlike the WTO DSB, none of these DSMs require that the parties to a dispute first attempt to resolve the dispute through consultation before seeking a solution through the use of other procedures.[45] Also, unlike the WTO DSB, none of these DSMs includes the principle contained in Article 33 of the UN Charter, which requires the parties to a dispute to seek a solution at the lowest adversarial level.[46]

---

[45] This WTO DSB provision is discussed in Section 12.4.4.

[46] This provision of the UN Charter is discussed in Section 12.3.1.

Abbreviations

ADD	Anti-dumping duties
AfCFTA	African Continental Free Trade Area
AHM	American Honda Motor Co., Inc.
APHIS	Animal and Plant Health Inspection Service of the USDA
ASEAN	Association of Southeast Asian Nations
ASEAN FTA	Association of Southeast Asian Nations Free Trade Area
AU	African Union
CBP	United States Customs and Border Protection
CCC	China Compulsory Certification
CCC	Customs Cooperation Council
CETA	Canada–EU Comprehensive Economic and Trade Agreement
CFIUS	Committee on Foreign Investment in the United States
CIS	Commonwealth of Independent States
CNCA	Certification and Accreditation Administration of China
CU	Customs union
CVD	Countervailing duty
DDTC	Directorate of Defense Trade Controls
DPW	Dubai Ports World
DSB	Dispute Settlement Body of the WTO
DSM	Dispute settlement mechanism
EAC	East Africa Community
ECOWAS	Economic Community of West African States
EEC	European Economic Community
EJV	Equity joint venture
EU	European Union
FDI	Foreign direct investment
FPI	Foreign portfolio investment
FSIS	Food Safety and Inspection Service of the USDA

FTA	Free trade agreement, free trade area
GATS	General Agreement on Trade in Services
GATT	General Agreement on Tariffs and Trade
GCC	Gulf Cooperation Council
HCCH	Hague Conference on Private International Law
HR	Human resources
HS	Harmonized System
HTSUS	Harmonized Tariff Schedule of the United States
HTSUSA	Harmonized Tariff Schedule of the United States Annotated
IBRD	International Bank for Reconstruction and Development (World Bank)
IC	International commerce
ICITO	Interim Commission for the International Trade Organization
ICJ	International Court of Justice (World Court)
ICSID	International Center for the Settlement of Investment Disputes
IMF	International Monetary Fund
IR	International relations
ISA	International strategic alliance
ISDS	Investor-State Dispute Settlement
ITI	Customs Convention on the International Transit of Goods
ITO	International trade organization
MA	Marrakesh Agreement, Agreement Establishing the WTO
MERCOSUR	Southern Cone Common Market
MFN	Most-favored-nation
MOU	Memoranda of understanding
NAFTA	North American Free Trade Agreement
NATO	North Atlantic Treaty Organization
NSGTs	Non-self-governing territories
NTB	Non-tariff barrier
OECD	Organization of Economic Cooperation and Development

P&O	Peninsular and Oriental Steam Navigation Company
PPA	Protocol of Provisional Application of the GATT
PTA	Preferential trade agreement
RCEP	Regional Comprehensive Economic Partnership
RIA	Regional integration agreement, regional integration area
ROO	Rules of origin
RTA	Regional trade agreement
RTB	Regional trade bloc, regional trading bloc
SAARC	South Asian Association for Regional Cooperation
SCM	Agreement on Subsidies and Countervailing Measures
SCO	Shanghai Cooperation Organization
SCT	Separate customs territory
SOE	State-owned enterprise
TBT	Technical barriers to trade
TPA	Trade promotion agreement
TRIMs	Agreement on Trade-Related Investment Measures
TRIPS	Agreement on Trade-Related Aspects of Intellectual Property Rights
TRQ	Tariff-rate quota
TSUS	Tariff Schedules of the United States
UAE	United Arab Emirates
UK	United Kingdom
UN	United Nations
UNCITRAL	United Nations Commission on International Trade and Law
UNCTAD	United Nations Conference on Trade and Development
UNESC	United Nations Economic and Social Committee
UNIDROIT	International Institute for the Unification of Private Law
US	United States
USDA	United States Department of Agriculture
USITC	United States International Trade Commission
USMCA	United States–Mexico–Canada Agreement
USML	United States Munitions List

USTR	United States Trade Representative
WCO	World Customs Organization
WIPO	World Intellectual Property Organization
WTO	World Trade Organization
WWII	Second World War

Bibliography

The bibliography for this book is available online at the book's web page. It is divided into two parts. "Part 1: Institutional sources," includes World Trade Organization sources, United Nations and UN Specialized Agencies sources, United States governmental sources, other governmental and intergovernmental sources, and non-governmental institutional sources. "Part 2" includes articles and books.

About the Authors

Warnock Davies holds MA, MALD, and PhD degrees in international law, international relations, and international trade from the Fletcher School of Law and Diplomacy at Tufts and Harvard Universities. He has worked as a senior-level consultant on international trade and FDI policies, strategies, initiatives, and issues with corporations and government departments in the United States and 40 other countries; has held full-time and visiting faculty appointments at universities in the United States and other countries; has directed and taught in graduate programs, university-based executive programs, and in-company seminars; and is the author of articles and books on strategy and international business.

Clive G. Chen holds BEc, BA, and MSc degrees in international economics, international trade, and international supply chain management from Shaoxing University, Coventry University, and Erasmus University Rotterdam. He is an international supply chain manager with Meelunie B.V., an Amsterdam-based trading company with operations in 105 countries, and regional offices in Australia, China, Mexico, Singapore, South Africa, and the United States. His operational areas of expertise include bilateral and multilateral preferential trade agreements, regional trade blocks, and technical barriers to trade and their effects on the conduct of international business.

The authors can be contacted at ITandFDI@outlook.com

Index

OTHER TITLES IN THE INTERNATIONAL BUSINESS COLLECTION

Tamer Cavusgil and Gary Knight, Editors

- *Strategic Development of Technology in China* by Kelly Luo
- *Adjusting to the New World Economy* by Michael Czinkota
- *Global Trends and Transformations in Culture, Business, and Technology* by Hamid Yeganeh
- *The Business of Relationships* by Joan Turley
- *The Chinese Market Series* by Danai Krokou
- *Trading With China* by Danai Krokou
- *The Chinese Market* by Danai Krokou
- *The Chinese e-Merging Market* by Danai Krokou
- *Creative Solutions to Global Business Negotiations, Third Edition* by Claude Cellich
- *Exporting* by Laurent Houlier and John Blaskey
- *Global Trade Strategies* by Michel Borgeon and Claude Cellich
- *Doing Business in Germany* by Andra Riemhofer

Concise and Applied Business Books

The Collection listed above is one of 30 business subject collections that Business Expert Press has grown to make BEP a premiere publisher of print and digital books. Our concise and applied books are for...

- Professionals and Practitioners
- Faculty who adopt our books for courses
- Librarians who know that BEP's Digital Libraries are a unique way to offer students ebooks to download, not restricted with any digital rights management
- Executive Training Course Leaders
- Business Seminar Organizers

Business Expert Press books are for anyone who needs to dig deeper on business ideas, goals, and solutions to everyday problems. Whether one print book, one ebook, or buying a digital library of 110 ebooks, we remain the affordable and smart way to be business smart. For more information, please visit www.businessexpertpress.com, or contact sales@businessexpertpress.com.

www.ingramcontent.com/pod-product-compliance
Lightning Source LLC
Chambersburg PA
CBHW061147220326
41599CB00025B/4388